STANDARDS FOR ELECTRONIC MONITORING PROGRAMS

American Correctional Association

in cooperation with the
Commission on Accreditation for Corrections

1995

American Correctional Association:

Standards for Adult Parole Authorities
Standards for Adult Correctional Boot Camp Facilities
Standards for Adult Community Residential Services
Standards for Adult Probation and Parole Field Services
Standards for Adult Correctional Institutions
Standards for Adult Local Detention Facilities
Standards for Juvenile Correctional Boot Camp Facilities
Standards for Juvenile Community Residential Facilities
Standards for Juvenile Probation and Aftercare Services
Standards for Juvenile Detention Facilities
Standards for Juvenile Training Schools
Standards for Small Juvenile Detention Facilities
Standards for Juvenile Day Treatment Programs
Standards for the Administration of Correctional Agencies
Standards for Correctional Training Academies
Standards for Electronic Monitoring Programs
Standards for Small Jail Facilities
Certification Standards for Health Care Programs
Certification Standards for Food Service Programs
Foundation/Core Standards for Adult Local Detention Facilities
Foundation/Core Standards for Adult Correctional Institutions
Foundation/Core Standards for Adult Community Residential Services
1994 Standards Supplement

This publication and others may be ordered from:

American Correctional Association
Division of Communications and Publications
8025 Laurel Lakes Court
Laurel, MD 20707-5075
1-800-825-BOOK

Information on accreditation may be obtained from:

American Correctional Association
Division of Standards and Accreditation
8025 Laurel Lakes Court
Laurel, MD 20707-5075
301-206-5044

All pictures on the cover are courtesy of Capitol Communications

American Correctional Association

*This manual and its contents were approved
during the administration of the following persons:*

Perry M. Johnson
President

James A. Gondles, Jr.
Executive Director

W. Hardy Rauch
Director, Standards and Accreditation

James R. Irving
Chair, Standards Committee

COMMISSION ON ACCREDITATION FOR CORRECTIONS

Acknowledgments

The development of standards that reflect contemporary correctional practice throughout the United States is not possible without the support, encouragement, dedication, and commitment of corrections professionals. We gratefully acknowledge the involvement of all those whose comments and suggestions contributed to the development of this publication including:

Robert L. Brutsche, M.D., Corrections Consultant, Alexandria, Virginia
Mike Dumovitch, Allvest, Inc., Granite Falls, Washington
Irene Favreau, Community Justice Coalition of Connecticut, Inc., Hartford
Den Freaney, President, Dismas Charities, Inc., Texas
Sue Gore, Topeka Halfway House, Topeka, Kansas
June Koegel, Executive Director, Volunteers of America of Maine, Portland
Anne McDiarmid, National Institute of Corrections, Washington, D.C.
Allen L. Patrick, FAIA, President, Patrick + Associates, Columbus, Ohio
Howard A. Peters III, Director, Illinois Department of Corrections, Springfield
Marc Renzema, Kutztown University, Kutztown, Pennsylvania
Bonnie Rogan, Executive Director, Isaiah 61:1 Incorporated, Bridgeport, Connecticut
John Simonet, Director of Corrections/Undersheriff, Denver Sheriff's Department, Denver, Colorado
Joe Vaughn, Central State Missouri University, Warrensburg, Missouri
Ray Wahl, Utah Department of Corrections, Salt Lake City
J. Christy Wareham, Linda Connelly & Associates, Inc., Monrovia, California
Jerome Weiner, CPM, Springfield, Massachusetts

We wish to give special recognition to the International Association of Residential and Community Alternatives (IARCA) including the following people who greatly contributed to this manual of Standards for Electronic Monitoring Programs:

Linda Connelly, President/CEO, Linda Connelly & Associates, Inc., San Francisco, California
Anne Schmidt, Federal Bureau of Prisons, Washington, D.C.
Peter Kinziger, Executive Director, IARCA, LaCrosse, Wisconsin

Introduction

Over the last two decades, sentencing alternatives have flourished as correctional systems have been overwhelmed by a growing number of offenders. The demand for meaningful sentences for low-risk offenders who can be served in the community has promulgated electronic monitoring into the continuum of community corrections sanctions.

Electronic monitoring was initiated ten years ago, but today represents a very small portion of community options. With the current overload in the criminal justice system, other options that provide opportunities for offenders to change, while maintaining public safety, must be pursued. Thus, it is expected that electronic monitoring will be used with greater regularity. In preparing for this, and to ensure that electronic monitoring becomes a viable component of community corrections, it is important to regulate and provide the field with a tool for guidance.

There are many types of programs in existence that cater to a variety of offender populations. Program philosophy varies significantly from state-to-state and county-to-county. Seemingly, this diversity in program type, size, and function would defy the uniformity of operations. Yet, it is clear that the formulation of operational guidelines would aid significantly in the development and operation of successful electronic monitoring programs.

The International Association of Residential and Community Alternatives (IARCA) instituted an electronic monitoring committee to define the needs of the field, provide research data, and write standards. It was important to write the standards as general guidelines, applicable to all program variations, for a front-end case or as a violation of probation or parole (whether programs are large or small, privately or publicly operated). The committee, chaired by Linda Connelly, solicited committee members from the private and public sector, along with representatives of the American Correctional Association. Many drafts of the standards were sent to probation offices, jails, departments of correction, manufacturers, and private operators for comment. Every effort was made to garner feedback in an attempt to provide standards that were comprehensive, realistic, and would promote program excellence.

After several rewrites, IARCA presented their draft to ACA in 1993, so that the standards could become a formal part of ACA's accreditation process. ACA realized that electronic monitoring needed greater regulation and should be part of the accreditation process and worked closely with IARCA's committee finalizing the draft. After further rewrites and editing by ACA, a final draft was presented to and approved by the ACA Standards Committee at the Congress of Correction held in St. Louis, Missouri, in August 1994.

The standards contained in this manual are guidelines for the comprehensive improvement of correctional programs. They provide a national framework for presenting the needs and concerns of electronic monitoring services to public officials, corrections administrators, legislators, funding agencies, and the public. The standards set high levels of compliance for agencies seeking to augment or upgrade their services, programs, and overall operation. The accreditation process provides the opportunity for public accountability through independent verification of performance. Nevertheless, the standards represent more than a tool for accreditation. They are to be used by correctional agencies as guidelines for self-improvement and as a stimulus for change at the legislative, executive, and judicial levels of government.

As time goes by and we learn more specifically the applicability of standards in electronic monitoring, revisions will be made that will unmistakenly illustrate their capacity to reflect changing views, based on new experience, additional knowledge, and expertise. This capacity to change and evolve through time is vital to the continued acceptance and use of the standards to improve correctional operations throughout the country.

The Accreditation Process

ACA and the Commission on Accreditation for Corrections (CAC) are private, nonprofit organizations that administer the only national accreditation program for all components of adult and juvenile corrections. Their purpose is to promote improvement in the management of correctional agencies through the administration of a voluntary accreditation program and the ongoing development and revision of relevant, useful standards.

Accreditation, a process that began in 1978, involves approximately 80 percent of all state departments of corrections and youth services as active participants. Also included are programs and facilities operated by the Federal Bureau of Prisons, the U.S. Parole Commission, and the District of Columbia. For these agencies, the accreditation program offers the opportunity to evaluate their operations against national standards, remedy deficiencies, and upgrade the quality of correctional programs and services. The recognized benefits from such a process include improved management, a defense against lawsuits through documentation and the demonstration of a "good faith" effort to improve conditions of confinement, increased accountability and enhanced public credibility for administrative and line staff, a safer and more humane environment for personnel and offenders, and the establishment of measurable criteria for upgrading programs, personnel, and the physical plant on a continuing basis.

The timelines, requirements, and outcomes of the accreditation process are the same for a state or federal prison, training school, local detention facility, private halfway house or group home, probation and parole field service agency, or paroling authority. All programs and facilities sign a contract, pay an accreditation fee, conduct a self evaluation, and have a standards compliance audit by trained ACA auditors before an accreditation decision is made by the Board of Commissioners. Once accredited, all programs and facilities submit annual certification statements to ACA. Also, at ACA's expense and discretion, a monitoring visit may be conducted during the initial three-year accreditation period to ensure continued compliance with the appropriate standards.

Participation in the Accreditation Process

Invitations to participate in the accreditation process have been extended to all adult and juvenile agencies for which standards have been developed and published. Participating agencies include public and private agencies; federal, state, and local agencies; and United States and Canadian correctional agencies.

Accreditation activities are initiated voluntarily by correctional administrators. When an agency chooses to pursue accreditation, ACA staff will provide the agency with appropriate information and application materials. These include a contract, the applicable manual of standards, a policy and procedure manual, and an organization summary (narrative).

Eligibility Criteria

To be eligible for accreditation, an agency must be a part of a governmental or private entity or conform to the applicable federal, state, and local laws and regulations regarding corporate existence. The agency must: (1) hold under confinement pretrial or presentence adults or juveniles who are being held pending a hearing for unlawful activity; or (2) hold under confinement sentenced adult offenders convicted of criminal activity or juveniles adjudicated to confinement; or (3) supervise in the community sentenced adult or adjudicated juvenile offenders, including juveniles placed in residential settings; and (4) have a single administrative officer responsible for agency operations. It is this administrative officer who makes formal application for admission for accreditation.

It is ACA's policy that nonadjudicated juveniles should be served outside the juvenile correctional system. Training schools housing status offenders must remove them before the facility can be awarded accreditation. Detention facilities may house status offenders who have violated valid court orders by continued perpetration of status offenses. In such instances, the following conditions would apply: status offenders are separated by sight and sound from delinquent offenders; facility staffs demonstrate attempts to mandate removal of all status offenders from detention centers; and special programs are developed for status offenders.

ACA does not prohibit community programs that house adjudicated juveniles with status offenders in nonsecure settings from participation in accreditation. However, ACA actively supports and requires exclusion of status offenders from the criminal and juvenile justice systems. Residential facilities and institutional programs that house adults and juveniles separated by sight and sound may become accredited. Individual cases may stipulate removal of juveniles before receiving an accreditation award.

Preaccreditation Assessment

Prior to signing an accreditation contract, an agency may request a preaccreditation assessment. The assessment requires an ACA auditor to visit the agency. The auditor will assess strengths and areas for improvement, measure readiness for application for accreditation, and identify steps required to achieve accreditation. A confidential, written report is provided to the agency to assist in making the decision to apply for accreditation.

Applicant Status

When the agency enters into the accreditation process, the administrator requests an information package from ACA. To confirm eligibility, determine appropriate fees, and schedule accreditation activities, the agency provides ACA with relevant narrative information through the organization summary. The Applicant Status begins when both the completed organization summary, which provides a written description of the facility/program, and the signed contract are returned to ACA. The Association will notify the agency of its acceptance into the accreditation process within 15 days of the receipt of the necessary application materials. ACA will then assign a regional administrator from the Division of Standards and Accreditation as a permanent liaison to the agency. The agency will appoint an accreditation manager, who will be responsible for organizing and supervising agency resources and activities to achieve accreditation.

As defined in the contract, the fees for the accreditation period cover all services normally provided to an agency by ACA staff, auditors, and the Board of Commissioners. The fees are determined during the application period and are included in the contract signed by the agency and ACA.

The fees for probation, parole, and aftercare field service agencies depend on the size, number, and locations of the field offices. The central office and a stipulated number of field offices are audited, with the fee determined by the number of auditor days and auditors required to complete the audit.

Correspondent Status

When the application is accepted, the agency enters into Correspondent Status. During this time, the agency conducts a self-assessment of its operations and completes a self-evaluation report, which specify the agency's level of standards compliance. (Self-evaluation reports are optional for facilities signing a reaccreditation contract.)

At the agency's request and expense, an on-site accreditation orientation for staff and/or a field consultation is scheduled. The object of the orientation is to prepare agency staff to complete the requirements of accreditation, including an understanding of self-evaluation activities, compilation of documentation, audit procedures, and standards interpretation. A field auditor provides information on accreditation policy and procedure, standards interpretations, and/or documentation requirements. Agency familiarity with standards and accreditation is the key factor in determining the need for these services.

The self-evaluation report includes the organizational summary, a compliance tally, preliminary requests for waivers or plans of action, and a completed standards compliance checklist for each standard in the applicable manual.

Applicable Standards

The standards used for accreditation address services, programs, and operations essential to good correctional management, including administrative, staff, and fiscal controls, staff training and development, physical plant, safety and emergency procedures, sanitation, food service, rules and discipline, and a variety of subjects that comprise good correctional practice. These standards are under continual revision to reflect changing practice, current case law, new knowledge, and agency experience with their application. These changes are published by ACA in the Standards Supplement.

ACA policy addresses the impact of the standards revisions on agencies involved in accreditation. Agencies signing contracts after the date that a Standards Supplement is published are held accountable for all standards changes in that supplement. Agencies are not held accountable for changes made after the contract is signed. The agencies may choose to apply new changes to the standards that have been issued following the program's entry into accreditation. Agencies must notify ACA of their decision before conducting the standards compliance audit.

Although accreditation is based only on ACA standards, provision is made for recognition of accreditation earned from the Joint Commission on Accreditation of Healthcare Organizations. This covers the accreditation of medical services in local detention facilities and Joint Commission accreditation of institutional hospital programs.

For accreditation purposes, any new architectural design, building, and/or renovation of the institution must be in accordance with the current standards manual at the time of the design, building, and/or renovation. In such cases, different standards would be applied to separate parts of the institution, respective to these changes in the physical plant.

Standards Compliance Checklist

In completing a standards compliance checklist, the agency checks compliance, noncompliance, or not applicable for each standard. Checking compliance signifies complete compliance with the content of the standard at all times and that the agency has documentation (primarily written) available to support compliance. A finding of noncompliance indicates that all or part of the requirements stated in the standard have not been met. A not applicable response means that the standard is clearly not relevant to the situation being audited. A written statement supporting nonapplicability of the standard is required.

At this time, the agency may request a waiver for one or more standards, provided that overall agency programming compensates for the lack of compliance. The waiver request must be accompanied by a clear explanation of the compensating conditions. The agency applies for a waiver only when the totality of conditions safeguard the life, health, and safety of offenders and staff. Waivers are not granted for standards designated as mandatory and do not change the conclusion of noncompliance or the agency's compliance tally. When a waiver is requested during the self-evaluation phase, ACA staff renders a preliminary judgement. A final decision can be made only by the Board of Commissioners during the accreditation hearing. Most waivers granted are for physical plant standards.

The Association requires that a self-evaluation report be completed by each applicant for accreditation. It is recommended that agencies entering into the accreditation process for the first time submit a written statement to ACA concerning their status at the completion of the evaluation. Information contained in this statement should include the percentage of compliance with mandatory and nonmandatory standards; a list of not applicable standards; and a list of noncompliant standards and their deficiencies. Within 60 days of receipt of this statement, ACA staff will provide the agency administrator with a written response containing, where appropriate, comments on materials or information submitted to the Association. The letter also provides notice to the agency of its acceptance to Candidate Status.

The compilation of written documentation requires the most time and effort during Correspondent Status. A separate documentation file, which explicitly shows compliance, is prepared for each standard.

In order to request an audit, an agency must comply with 100 percent of the standards designated as mandatory and 90 percent of the nonmandatory standards. (The self-evaluation report does not necessarily need to reflect these levels of compliance.)

Candidate Status

The agency enters into Candidate Status with ACA's acceptance of the self-evaluation report or agency certification of its completion. Candidate Status continues until the agency meets the required level of compliance, has been audited by a visiting committee composed of ACA auditors, and has been awarded or denied a three-year accreditation by the Board of Commissioners. Candidate Status lasts up to 12 months.

An agency may request, in writing, an extension of Candidate Status stating the reasons for the request. ACA staff considers the request and renders a decision. It is ACA policy that extensions of Candidate Status may not exceed 12 months.

The agency requests a standards compliance audit when the facility administrator believes the agency or facility has met or exceeded the compliance levels required for accreditation (100 percent mandatory; 90 percent nonmandatory).

Standards Compliance Audit

The agency's request for an audit is made six to eight weeks before the desired audit dates. The purpose of the audit is to have the visiting committee measure the agency's operation against the standards based on the documentation provided by the agency. A visiting committee completes the audit and prepares a visiting committee report for submission to the Commission. ACA designates a visiting committee chair to organize and supervise the committee's activities.

Prior to arrival at the audit site, each member of the visiting committee reviews the agency's descriptive narrative and any additional information that ACA may have provided, including pending litigation and court orders submitted by the agency and any inmate correspondence. The visiting committee chair makes audit assignments to each auditor. For example, one auditor may audit the administrative, fiscal, and personnel standards, while another audits standards for physical plant, sanitation, and security. Upon arrival, the visiting committee meets with the administrator, accreditation manager, and other appropriate staff to discuss the scope of the audit and the schedule of activities. This exchange of information provides for the development of an audit schedule that ensures the least amount of disruption to routine agency operation.

The exact amount of time required to complete the audit depends on agency size, number of applicable standards, additional facilities to be audited, and the accessibility and organization of documentation. To hasten the audit, all documentation should be clearly referenced and located where the visiting committee is to work.

The accreditation manager's responsibilities include compiling and making accessible to all visiting committee members the standards compliance documentation and release of information forms for personnel and offender records. Also, staff should be notified beforehand to ensure that they are available to discuss specific issues or conduct tours of the facility for the visiting committee.

During the audit, the members of the visiting committee tour the facility, review documentation prepared for each standard, and interview staff and offenders to make compliance decisions. The visiting committee reports its findings on the same standards compliance checklist used by the agency in preparing its self-evaluation report. All members of the visiting committee review all mandatory standards, all areas of noncompliance and nonapplicability, and all requests for waivers, with decisions made collectively. (Final decisions on waivers can be approved only by the Commission at the time of the agency's accreditation hearing.)

Interviewing staff members and offenders is an integral part of the audit. In addition to speaking with those who request an interview with the team, the members of the visiting committee select other individuals to interview and to discuss issues. Interviews are voluntary and occur randomly throughout the audit, and those interviewed are ensured that their discussions are confidential.

In addition to auditing standards documentation, auditors will evaluate the quality of life or conditions of confinement. An acceptable quality of life is necessary for an agency to be eligible for accreditation. Factors that the visiting committee consider include: the adequacy and quality of programs, activities, and services available to juveniles and their involvement; occurrences of disturbances, serious incidents, assaults, or violence, including their frequency and methods of dealing with them to ensure the safety of staff and juveniles; and overall physical conditions, including conditions of confinement, program space, and institutional maintenance related to sanitation, health, and safety.

At the conclusion of the audit, the visiting committee again meets with the administrator, the accreditation manager, and any others selected by the administrator to discuss the results of the audit. During this exit interview, the visiting committee reports the standards compliance tally and all findings of noncompliance and nonapplicability, as well as preliminary decisions on waivers, stating the reasons for each decision.

If the visiting committee finds that the agency is in noncompliance with one or more mandatory standards or does not meet sufficient nonmandatory standards compliance levels to be considered for accreditation, the chair advises the agency that an on-site supplemental audit may be required prior to scheduling an accreditation hearing. The agency is responsible for notifying ACA when the deficiencies have been corrected and a supplemental audit is desired. The agency bears the cost of the supplemental audit. An ACA auditor, often a member of the original visiting committee, returns to the agency to reaudit the appropriate standards. The visiting committee report includes the written report from the supplemental audit.

The chair of the visiting committee then prepares and submits a copy of the visiting committee report to ACA staff within ten days of the completion of the audit. ACA staff review the report for completeness, enters the data, and within 15 days of the audit's completion, it is submitted to the agency administrator and other members of the visiting committee for concurrence. Upon receipt of the visiting committee report, the agency has 15 days to submit its written response to the report to ACA staff and all members of the visiting committee.

The Accreditation Hearing

The CAC Board of Commissioners is responsible for rendering accreditation decisions and is divided into accreditation panels authorized to render such decisions. Panels meet separately, or with a full board meeting, and are composed of three to five commissioners.

The agency is invited to have representation at the accreditation hearing. Unless circumstances dictate otherwise, a member of the visiting committee is not present; however, an ACA staff member does participate. At the accreditation hearing, the agency representative provides information about the agency, speaks in support of its appeal and/or waiver requests, and addresses concerns the panel may have with regards to the accreditation application.

After completing its review, the accreditation panel votes to award or deny accreditation or continue the agency in Candidate Status. When an agency receives a three-year accreditation award, a certificate with the effective date of the award is presented to the agency representative.

The Board of Commissioners may stipulate additional requirements for accreditation if, in its opinion, conditions exist in the facility or program that adversely affect the life, health, or safety of the staff or offenders. These requests are specific regarding activities required and timelines for their completion. The panel advises the agency representative of all changes at the time the accreditation decision is made.

ACA and the Commission may deny accreditation for insufficient standards compliance, inadequate plans of action, or failure to meet other requirements as determined by the Board of Commissioners, including, but not limited to, the conditions of confinement in a given facility. In not awarding accreditation, the Commission may extend an agency in Candidate Status for a specified period of time and for identified deficiencies, if in its judgement the agency is actively pursuing compliance. Those agencies denied accreditation, but not extended in Candidate Status, may reapply for accreditation after 180 days. The agency receives written notification of all decisions relative to its accreditation following the accreditation hearing.

Accredited Status

During the three-year accreditation period, ACA requires that accredited agencies submit annual certification statements confirming continued standards compliance at levels necessary for accreditation. The report should include the agency's progress on completing plans of action and other significant events that may affect the accreditation award. In addition, ACA may require accredited agencies to submit written responses to public criticism, notoriety, or patterns of complaints about agency activity that suggest a failure to maintain standards compliance. The Association, at its own expense and with advance notice, may conduct on-site monitoring visits to verify continued standards compliance or conditions of confinement.

Reconsideration Process

The goal of ACA's accreditation process is to ensure the equity, fairness, and reliability of its decisions, particularly those that constitute either denial or revocation of Accredited Status. Therefore, an agency may request reconsideration of any denial or revocation of accreditation. However, the reasonableness of ACA's standards, criteria, and/or procedures for accreditation may not serve as the basis for reconsideration.

A reconsideration request is based on the grounds that the adverse decision is (1) arbitrary, erratic, or otherwise in substantial disregard of the criteria and/or procedures for accreditation as stated by ACA, (2) based on incorrect facts or an incorrect interpretation of facts, or (3) unsupported substantial evidence.

The agency submits a written request for reconsideration to ACA staff within 30 days of the adverse decision stating the basis for the request. The Commission's Executive Committee reviews the request and decides whether there is sufficient evidence to warrant a reconsideration hearing before the Board of Commissioners. The agency is notified in writing of the Executive Committee's decision.

Revocation of Accreditation

An accredited agency that does not maintain the required levels of compliance throughout the three-year accreditation period, including continuous compliance with all mandatory standards, may have its accreditation award revoked. The agency is notified of its deficiencies and given a specified amount of time to correct them. If the deficiencies continue, the Board of Commissioners may place the agency on Probationary Status for an additional stated period of time and require documentation of compliance. Should the agency fail to correct the deficiencies, the Board of Commissioners may revoke the agency's accreditation and request that the Accreditation Certificate be returned to ACA. An accredited agency that has had its accreditation revoked for reasons of noncompliance also may use the reconsideration process.

Reaccreditation

To ensure continuous Accredited Status, accredited agencies should apply for reaccreditation approximately 12 months before the expiration of their current accreditation award. Agencies have the option of being audited from individual accreditation files or operational files. For detailed information on reaccreditation, consult your ACA regional administrator.

The preceding information is provided as an overview of the accreditation process. Additional information on specific procedures and elements of the process is available from ACA's Standards and Accreditation Department.

Table of Contents

Appendices (Continued)

STANDARDS FOR
ELECTRONIC MONITORING PROGRAMS

Totals of Weights

Category	Number
Mandatory Standards	3
Nonmandatory Standards	<u>124</u>
Total	127

Summary of Mandatory Standards

1-EM-1F-10	Offender Participation in Research
1-EM-2A-03	Fire Codes
1-EM-3B-05	Flammable, Toxic, and Caustic Materials

Part One
Administration and Management

Section A
General Administration

Principle: A written body of policy and procedure establishes the program's goals, objectives, and standard operating procedures and provides for a system of regular review.

Purpose and Mission

1-EM-1A-01   **The public or private agency operating an electronic monitoring program is a legal entity or a part of a legal entity.**

Comment:
None.

SELF-EVALUATION Agency Personnel	STANDARDS COMPLIANCE AUDIT Visiting Committee
Staff Signature(s): _____ _____ ❑ Compliance (list documentation) ❑ Noncompliance (see plan of action) ❑ Not applicable (justification attached) ❑ Plan of action waiver requested (justification attached) Prepare one of the following, as appropriate: 1) List documentation to support compliance; 2) Explain nonapplicability of standard: 3) Explain plan of action waiver request.	Auditor Signature(s): _____ _____ ❑ Compliance ❑ POA acceptable ❑ Noncompliance ❑ POA unacceptable ❑ Not Applicable ❑ Waiver acceptable ❑ Waiver unacceptable List deficiencies if standard is in noncompliance: **NOTE: List all deficiencies if standard is in noncompliance or not applicable. State exactly why standard is in noncompliance. Make complete comments in space above and attach any other information, if necessary. BE VERY SPECIFIC!**

1-EM-1A-02   **Written policy, procedure, and practice provide that the agency meets periodic filing requirements necessary to maintain its legal authority to continue operations (private agencies only).**

Comment:
Many state and local jurisdictions require private organizations to file financial reports or renew licenses.

SELF-EVALUATION Agency Personnel	STANDARDS COMPLIANCE AUDIT Visiting Committee

Staff Signature(s):

_____

_____

❏ Compliance (list documentation)
❏ Noncompliance (see plan of action)
❏ Not applicable (justification attached)
❏ Plan of action waiver requested (justification attached)

Prepare one of the following, as appropriate:

1) List documentation to support compliance;
2) Explain nonapplicability of standard:
3) Explain plan of action waiver request.

Auditor Signature(s):

_____

_____

❏ Compliance   ❏ POA acceptable
❏ Noncompliance   ❏ POA unacceptable
❏ Not Applicable   ❏ Waiver acceptable
                          ❏ Waiver unacceptable

List deficiencies if standard is in noncompliance:

NOTE: List all deficiencies if standard is in noncompliance or not applicable. State exactly why standard is in noncompliance. Make complete comments in space above and attach any other information, if necessary. BE VERY SPECIFIC!

Policy and Goal Formulation

1-EM-1A-03 **Written policy, procedure, and practice demonstrate that employees participate in the formulation of policies, procedures, and programs.**

Comment:
Employee participation can be achieved through meetings, reports, employee councils, and/or correspondence.

SELF-EVALUATION **Agency Personnel**	**STANDARDS COMPLIANCE AUDIT** **Visiting Committee**
Staff Signature(s): _____ _____	Auditor Signature(s): _____ _____

SELF-EVALUATION — Agency Personnel

❑ Compliance (list documentation)
❑ Noncompliance (see plan of action)
❑ Not applicable (justification attached)
❑ Plan of action waiver requested (justification attached)

Prepare one of the following, as appropriate:

1) List documentation to support compliance;
2) Explain nonapplicability of standard:
3) Explain plan of action waiver request.

STANDARDS COMPLIANCE AUDIT — Visiting Committee

❑ Compliance   ❑ POA acceptable
❑ Noncompliance   ❑ POA unacceptable
❑ Not Applicable ❑ Waiver acceptable
                  ❑ Waiver unacceptable

List deficiencies if standard is in noncompliance:

NOTE: List all deficiencies if standard is in noncompliance or not applicable. State exactly why standard is in noncompliance. Make complete comments in space above and attach any other information, if necessary. BE VERY SPECIFIC!

1-EM-1A-04   **Written policy, procedure, and practice provide that the program has documented long-range goals and objectives that are reviewed at least annually and updated as needed.**

Comment:
Administrators should set forth long-term goals and objectives that are assessed periodically to ensure that appropriate action is being taken to achieve these goals.

SELF-EVALUATION Agency Personnel	STANDARDS COMPLIANCE AUDIT Visiting Committee
Staff Signature(s): _____ _____ ❑ Compliance (list documentation) ❑ Noncompliance (see plan of action) ❑ Not applicable (justification attached) ❑ Plan of action waiver requested (justification attached) Prepare one of the following, as appropriate: 1) List documentation to support compliance; 2) Explain nonapplicability of standard: 3) Explain plan of action waiver request.	Auditor Signature(s): _____ _____ ❑ Compliance ❑ POA acceptable ❑ Noncompliance ❑ POA unacceptable ❑ Not Applicable ❑ Waiver acceptable ❑ Waiver unacceptable List deficiencies if standard is in noncompliance: **NOTE: List all deficiencies if standard is in noncompliance or not applicable. State exactly why standard is in noncompliance. Make complete comments in space above and attach any other information, if necessary. BE VERY SPECIFIC!**

Qualifications

1-EM-1A-05   **Written policy, procedure, and practice provide that the program is managed by a single administrative officer.**

Comment:
None.

SELF-EVALUATION Agency Personnel	STANDARDS COMPLIANCE AUDIT Visiting Committee
Staff Signature(s): _____ _____ ❏ Compliance (list documentation) ❏ Noncompliance (see plan of action) ❏ Not applicable (justification attached) ❏ Plan of action waiver requested (justification attached) Prepare one of the following, as appropriate: 1) List documentation to support compliance; 2) Explain nonapplicability of standard: 3) Explain plan of action waiver request.	Auditor Signature(s): _____ _____ ❏ Compliance ❏ POA acceptable ❏ Noncompliance ❏ POA unacceptable ❏ Not Applicable ❏ Waiver acceptable ❏ Waiver unacceptable List deficiencies if standard is in noncompliance: **NOTE: List all deficiencies if standard is in noncompliance or not applicable. State exactly why standard is in noncompliance. Make complete comments in space above and attach any other information, if necessary. BE VERY SPECIFIC!**

Table of Organization

1-EM-1A-06   **There is a written document that describes the program's organization. The description includes an organizational chart that groups similar functions, services, and activities in administrative subunits. The chart is reviewed at least annually and updated, if needed.**

Comment:
A current organizational chart is necessary to provide a clear administrative picture. The chart should reflect span of control, lines of authority, and an orderly channel of communication.

SELF-EVALUATION Agency Personnel	STANDARDS COMPLIANCE AUDIT Visiting Committee
Staff Signature(s): _____ _____ ❑ Compliance (list documentation) ❑ Noncompliance (see plan of action) ❑ Not applicable (justification attached) ❑ Plan of action waiver requested (justification attached) Prepare one of the following, as appropriate: 1) List documentation to support compliance; 2) Explain nonapplicability of standard: 3) Explain plan of action waiver request.	Auditor Signature(s): _____ _____ ❑ Compliance ❑ POA acceptable ❑ Noncompliance ❑ POA unacceptable ❑ Not Applicable ❑ Waiver acceptable ❑ Waiver unacceptable List deficiencies if standard is in noncompliance: **NOTE: List all deficiencies if standard is in noncompliance or not applicable. State exactly why standard is in noncompliance. Make complete comments in space above and attach any other information, if necessary. BE VERY SPECIFIC!**

Role of Outside Agencies

1-EM-1A-07   **Written policy, procedure, and practice provide for communication and cooperation with community agencies and other components of the criminal justice system.**

Comment:
None.

SELF-EVALUATION Agency Personnel	STANDARDS COMPLIANCE AUDIT Visiting Committee
Staff Signature(s): _____ _____ ❑ Compliance (list documentation) ❑ Noncompliance (see plan of action) ❑ Not applicable (justification attached) ❑ Plan of action waiver requested (justification attached) Prepare one of the following, as appropriate: 1) List documentation to support compliance; 2) Explain nonapplicability of standard: 3) Explain plan of action waiver request.	Auditor Signature(s): _____ _____ ❑ Compliance ❑ POA acceptable ❑ Noncompliance ❑ POA unacceptable ❑ Not Applicable ❑ Waiver acceptable ❑ Waiver unacceptable List deficiencies if standard is in noncompliance: **NOTE: List all deficiencies if standard is in noncompliance or not applicable. State exactly why standard is in noncompliance. Make complete comments in space above and attach any other information, if necessary. BE VERY SPECIFIC!**

1-EM-1A-08   **The program has an advisory board that is representative of the community in which it is located that meets at least annually.**

Comment:
The board should be a link between the program and the community it serves.

SELF-EVALUATION Agency Personnel	STANDARDS COMPLIANCE AUDIT Visiting Committee
Staff Signature(s): _____ _____	Auditor Signature(s): _____ _____

❏ Compliance (list documentation) ❏ Noncompliance (see plan of action) ❏ Not applicable (justification attached) ❏ Plan of action waiver requested (justification attached)	❏ Compliance ❏ POA acceptable ❏ Noncompliance ❏ POA unacceptable ❏ Not Applicable ❏ Waiver acceptable ❏ Waiver unacceptable

Prepare one of the following, as appropriate:

1) List documentation to support compliance;
2) Explain nonapplicability of standard:
3) Explain plan of action waiver request.

List deficiencies if standard is in noncompliance:

NOTE: List all deficiencies if standard is in noncompliance or not applicable. State exactly why standard is in noncompliance. Make complete comments in space above and attach any other information, if necessary. BE VERY SPECIFIC!

1-EM-1A-09   **Written policy, procedure, and practice provide for operating and maintaining the program as specified in a manual that is accessible to all employees.**

Comment:
None.

SELF-EVALUATION Agency Personnel	STANDARDS COMPLIANCE AUDIT Visiting Committee
Staff Signature(s):	Auditor Signature(s):

❑ Compliance (list documentation) ❑ Noncompliance (see plan of action) ❑ Not applicable (justification attached) ❑ Plan of action waiver requested (justification attached)	❑ Compliance ❑ POA acceptable ❑ Noncompliance ❑ POA unacceptable ❑ Not Applicable ❑ Waiver acceptable ❑ Waiver unacceptable
Prepare one of the following, as appropriate: 1) List documentation to support compliance; 2) Explain nonapplicability of standard: 3) Explain plan of action waiver request.	List deficiencies if standard is in noncompliance:
	NOTE: List all deficiencies if standard is in noncompliance or not applicable. State exactly why standard is in noncompliance. Make complete comments in space above and attach any other information, if necessary. BE VERY SPECIFIC!

1-EM-1A-10   **Written policy, procedure, and practice provide that policies are reviewed at least annually and that new or revised policies and procedures are disseminated to designated staff and volunteers.**

Comment:
Dissemination of policies and procedures increases the effectiveness of the program's communication system.

SELF-EVALUATION Agency Personnel	STANDARDS COMPLIANCE AUDIT Visiting Committee
Staff Signature(s): _____ _____ ❑ Compliance (list documentation) ❑ Noncompliance (see plan of action) ❑ Not applicable (justification attached) ❑ Plan of action waiver requested (justification attached) Prepare one of the following, as appropriate: 1) List documentation to support compliance; 2) Explain nonapplicability of standard: 3) Explain plan of action waiver request.	Auditor Signature(s): _____ _____ ❑ Compliance ❑ POA acceptable ❑ Noncompliance ❑ POA unacceptable ❑ Not Applicable ❑ Waiver acceptable ❑ Waiver unacceptable List deficiencies if standard is in noncompliance: **NOTE: List all deficiencies if standard is in noncompliance or not applicable. State exactly why standard is in noncompliance. Make complete comments in space above and attach any other information, if necessary. BE VERY SPECIFIC!**

Channels of Communication

1-EM-1A-11   **Written policy, procedure, and practice provide that the program administrator attends meetings of the governing authority at least annually to facilitate communication, establish policy, and ensure conformity with legal and fiscal requirements.**

Comment:
Annual meetings are an excellent technique to ensure that principal staff members are following the policies of the governing authority. They also provide the governing authority with an opportunity to review and evaluate the operation.

SELF-EVALUATION Agency Personnel	STANDARDS COMPLIANCE AUDIT Visiting Committee
Staff Signature(s):	Auditor Signature(s):
_____ _____	_____
❑ Compliance (list documentation) ❑ Noncompliance (see plan of action) ❑ Not applicable (justification attached) ❑ Plan of action waiver requested (justification attached) Prepare one of the following, as appropriate: 1) List documentation to support compliance; 2) Explain nonapplicability of standard: 3) Explain plan of action waiver request.	❑ Compliance ❑ POA acceptable ❑ Noncompliance ❑ POA unacceptable ❑ Not Applicable ❑ Waiver acceptable ❑ Waiver unacceptable List deficiencies if standard is in noncompliance: **NOTE: List all deficiencies if standard is in noncompliance or not applicable. State exactly why standard is in noncompliance. Make complete comments in space above and attach any other information, if necessary. BE VERY SPECIFIC!**

1-EM-1A-12   **Written policy, procedure, and practice provide for regular meetings, at least monthly, between the program administrator and key staff members.**

Comment:
Regular channels of communication are necessary for delegating authority, assigning responsibility, supervising work, and coordinating efforts.

SELF-EVALUATION Agency Personnel	STANDARDS COMPLIANCE AUDIT Visiting Committee
Staff Signature(s): _____ _____ ❑ Compliance (list documentation) ❑ Noncompliance (see plan of action) ❑ Not applicable (justification attached) ❑ Plan of action waiver requested (justification attached) Prepare one of the following, as appropriate: 1) List documentation to support compliance; 2) Explain nonapplicability of standard: 3) Explain plan of action waiver request.	Auditor Signature(s): _____ _____ ❑ Compliance ❑ POA acceptable ❑ Noncompliance ❑ POA unacceptable ❑ Not Applicable ❑ Waiver acceptable ❑ Waiver unacceptable List deficiencies if standard is in noncompliance: **NOTE: List all deficiencies if standard is in noncompliance or not applicable. State exactly why standard is in noncompliance. Make complete comments in space above and attach any other information, if necessary. BE VERY SPECIFIC!**

1-EM-1A-13   **Written policy, procedure, and practice provide for a system of communication between all levels of staff and offenders.**

Comment:
None.

SELF-EVALUATION Agency Personnel	STANDARDS COMPLIANCE AUDIT Visiting Committee
Staff Signature(s): _____ _____ ❑ Compliance (list documentation) ❑ Noncompliance (see plan of action) ❑ Not applicable (justification attached) ❑ Plan of action waiver requested (justification attached) Prepare one of the following, as appropriate: 1) List documentation to support compliance; 2) Explain nonapplicability of standard: 3) Explain plan of action waiver request.	Auditor Signature(s): _____ _____ ❑ Compliance ❑ POA acceptable ❑ Noncompliance ❑ POA unacceptable ❑ Not Applicable ❑ Waiver acceptable ❑ Waiver unacceptable List deficiencies if standard is in noncompliance: **NOTE: List all deficiencies if standard is in noncompliance or not applicable. State exactly why standard is in noncompliance. Make complete comments in space above and attach any other information, if necessary. BE VERY SPECIFIC!**

Monitoring and Assessment

1-EM-1A-14   **Written policy, procedure, and practice provide for an internal system for monitoring programs through inspections or reviews conducted by the program administrator or designated staff. Reviews are held at least annually or as stipulated by statute or regulation.**

Comment:
Operations and programs should be implemented as outlined in policies and procedures. An audit system providing timely and periodic assessment of the various agency operations will reveal the degree of compliance. The internal administrative audit should exist apart from any external or continuing audit conducted by other agencies.

SELF-EVALUATION Agency Personnel	STANDARDS COMPLIANCE AUDIT Visiting Committee
Staff Signature(s): _____ _____	Auditor Signature(s): _____ _____
❑ Compliance (list documentation) ❑ Noncompliance (see plan of action) ❑ Not applicable (justification attached) ❑ Plan of action waiver requested (justification attached) Prepare one of the following, as appropriate: 1) List documentation to support compliance; 2) Explain nonapplicability of standard: 3) Explain plan of action waiver request.	❑ Compliance ❑ POA acceptable ❑ Noncompliance ❑ POA unacceptable ❑ Not Applicable ❑ Waiver acceptable ❑ Waiver unacceptable List deficiencies if standard is in noncompliance: **NOTE: List all deficiencies if standard is in noncompliance or not applicable. State exactly why standard is in noncompliance. Make complete comments in space above and attach any other information, if necessary. BE VERY SPECIFIC!**

1-EM-1A-15 **Written policy, procedure, and practice provide that a report of the program's activities is prepared at least annually and provided to appropriate persons, agencies, and, upon request, the public consistent with offenders' rights to confidentiality and privacy.**

Comment:
It is a good practice for the program to keep the public informed and aware of its activities and role in the community. Both public and private agencies should prepare a report that reviews its activities and gives statistical data and financial information.

SELF-EVALUATION Agency Personnel	STANDARDS COMPLIANCE AUDIT Visiting Committee
Staff Signature(s): _____ _____ ❏ Compliance (list documentation) ❏ Noncompliance (see plan of action) ❏ Not applicable (justification attached) ❏ Plan of action waiver requested (justification attached) Prepare one of the following, as appropriate: 1) List documentation to support compliance; 2) Explain nonapplicability of standard: 3) Explain plan of action waiver request.	Auditor Signature(s): _____ _____ ❏ Compliance ❏ POA acceptable ❏ Noncompliance ❏ POA unacceptable ❏ Not Applicable ❏ Waiver acceptable ❏ Waiver unacceptable List deficiencies if standard is in noncompliance: **NOTE: List all deficiencies if standard is in noncompliance or not applicable. State exactly why standard is in noncompliance. Make complete comments in space above and attach any other information, if necessary. BE VERY SPECIFIC!**

Public/Media Information

1-EM-1A-16 **Written policy, procedure, and practice provide for a public information program that encourages interaction with the public and the news media.**

Comment:
A continuing public information program helps to communicate the program's goals and objectives and to foster community involvement and support. The program should take into account the need to preserve the confidentiality of individual offender cases.

SELF-EVALUATION Agency Personnel	STANDARDS COMPLIANCE AUDIT Visiting Committee
Staff Signature(s): _____ _____	Auditor Signature(s): _____ _____

SELF-EVALUATION	STANDARDS COMPLIANCE AUDIT
❑ Compliance (list documentation) ❑ Noncompliance (see plan of action) ❑ Not applicable (justification attached) ❑ Plan of action waiver requested (justification attached) Prepare one of the following, as appropriate: 1) List documentation to support compliance; 2) Explain nonapplicability of standard: 3) Explain plan of action waiver request.	❑ Compliance ❑ POA acceptable ❑ Noncompliance ❑ POA unacceptable ❑ Not Applicable ❑ Waiver acceptable ❑ Waiver unacceptable List deficiencies if standard is in noncompliance: **NOTE: List all deficiencies if standard is in noncompliance or not applicable. State exactly why standard is in noncompliance. Make complete comments in space above and attach any other information, if necessary. BE VERY SPECIFIC!**

Legal Counsel

1-EM-1A-17 **Written policy, procedure, and practice provide that legal assistance is available to staff as required in the performance of their duties.**

Comment:
Qualified legal assistance is necessary to ensure that policies and procedures are consistent with relevant court decisions. Legal counsel also can advise on meeting statutory and court requirements, program operations, and individual cases and provide representation before courts and other bodies. Counsel should be available promptly and continuously.

SELF-EVALUATION Agency Personnel	STANDARDS COMPLIANCE AUDIT Visiting Committee
Staff Signature(s):	Auditor Signature(s):
_____	_____
_____	_____
❑ Compliance (list documentation) ❑ Noncompliance (see plan of action) ❑ Not applicable (justification attached) ❑ Plan of action waiver requested (justification attached)	❑ Compliance ❑ POA acceptable ❑ Noncompliance ❑ POA unacceptable ❑ Not Applicable ❑ Waiver acceptable ❑ Waiver unacceptable
Prepare one of the following, as appropriate: 1) List documentation to support compliance; 2) Explain nonapplicability of standard: 3) Explain plan of action waiver request.	List deficiencies if standard is in noncompliance: **NOTE: List all deficiencies if standard is in noncompliance or not applicable. State exactly why standard is in noncompliance. Make complete comments in space above and attach any other information, if necessary. BE VERY SPECIFIC!**

Political Practices

1-EM-1A-18   **Written policy, procedure, and practice provides conformance with governmental statutes and regulations relating to campaigning, lobbying, and political practices.**

Comment:
None.

SELF-EVALUATION Agency Personnel	STANDARDS COMPLIANCE AUDIT Visiting Committee
Staff Signature(s): _____ _____ ❑ Compliance (list documentation) ❑ Noncompliance (see plan of action) ❑ Not applicable (justification attached) ❑ Plan of action waiver requested (justification attached) Prepare one of the following, as appropriate: 1) List documentation to support compliance; 2) Explain nonapplicability of standard: 3) Explain plan of action waiver request.	Auditor Signature(s): _____ _____ ❑ Compliance ❑ POA acceptable ❑ Noncompliance ❑ POA unacceptable ❑ Not Applicable ❑ Waiver acceptable ❑ Waiver unacceptable List deficiencies if standard is in noncompliance: **NOTE: List all deficiencies if standard is in noncompliance or not applicable. State exactly why standard is in noncompliance. Make complete comments in space above and attach any other information, if necessary. BE VERY SPECIFIC!**

Conflict of Interest

1-EM-1A-19   **The program has a written policy concerning conflict of interest.**

Comment:
In order to protect the integrity of the program, a policy must exist that prohibits any possible conflict of interest between the program, its governing body, funding source, staff, volunteers, and/or board members.

SELF-EVALUATION Agency Personnel	STANDARDS COMPLIANCE AUDIT Visiting Committee
Staff Signature(s):	Auditor Signature(s):
_____ _____	_____ _____

SELF-EVALUATION — Agency Personnel:

❑ Compliance (list documentation)
❑ Noncompliance (see plan of action)
❑ Not applicable (justification attached)
❑ Plan of action waiver requested (justification attached)

Prepare one of the following, as appropriate:

1) List documentation to support compliance;
2) Explain nonapplicability of standard:
3) Explain plan of action waiver request.

STANDARDS COMPLIANCE AUDIT — Visiting Committee:

❑ Compliance   ❑ POA acceptable
❑ Noncompliance   ❑ POA unacceptable
❑ Not Applicable   ❑ Waiver acceptable
                              ❑ Waiver unacceptable

List deficiencies if standard is in noncompliance:

NOTE: List all deficiencies if standard is in noncompliance or not applicable. State exactly why standard is in noncompliance. Make complete comments in space above and attach any other information, if necessary. BE VERY SPECIFIC!

Program Differentiation

1-EM-1A-20   **Written policy, procedure, and practice provide that programs serving both juveniles and adults have written statements of philosophy, policy, program, and procedure that distinguish between criminal codes and the statutes that establish and give direction to programs for juveniles.**

Comment:
None.

SELF-EVALUATION Agency Personnel	STANDARDS COMPLIANCE AUDIT Visiting Committee
Staff Signature(s): _____ _____ ❑ Compliance (list documentation) ❑ Noncompliance (see plan of action) ❑ Not applicable (justification attached) ❑ Plan of action waiver requested (justification attached) Prepare one of the following, as appropriate: 1) List documentation to support compliance; 2) Explain nonapplicability of standard: 3) Explain plan of action waiver request.	Auditor Signature(s): _____ _____ ❑ Compliance ❑ POA acceptable ❑ Noncompliance ❑ POA unacceptable ❑ Not Applicable ❑ Waiver acceptable ❑ Waiver unacceptable List deficiencies if standard is in noncompliance: **NOTE: List all deficiencies if standard is in noncompliance or not applicable. State exactly why standard is in noncompliance. Make complete comments in space above and attach any other information, if necessary. BE VERY SPECIFIC!**

Private Agencies Only

1-EM-1A-21   **At a minimum, the bylaws for the governing authority of the agency include:**

- **membership (types, qualifications, community representation, rights, duties)**
- **size of governing body**
- **method of selection**
- **terms of office**
- **duties and responsibilities of officers**
- **times authority will meet**
- **committees**
- **parliamentary procedures**
- **recording of minutes**
- **method of amending the bylaws**
- **conflict of interest provisions**

Comment:
None.

SELF-EVALUATION Agency Personnel	STANDARDS COMPLIANCE AUDIT Visiting Committee
Staff Signature(s): _____ _____	Auditor Signature(s): _____ _____
❑ Compliance (list documentation) ❑ Noncompliance (see plan of action) ❑ Not applicable (justification attached) ❑ Plan of action waiver requested (justification attached) Prepare one of the following, as appropriate: 1) List documentation to support compliance; 2) Explain nonapplicability of standard: 3) Explain plan of action waiver request.	❑ Compliance ❑ POA acceptable ❑ Noncompliance ❑ POA unacceptable ❑ Not Applicable ❑ Waiver acceptable ❑ Waiver unacceptable List deficiencies if standard is in noncompliance: **NOTE: List all deficiencies if standard is in noncompliance or not applicable. State exactly why standard is in noncompliance. Make complete comments in space above and attach any other information, if necessary. BE VERY SPECIFIC!**

Section B
Fiscal Management

Principle: A written body of policy and procedure establishes the program's fiscal planning, budgeting, and accounting procedures and provides a system of regular review.

Fiscal Control

1-EM-1B-01   **Written policy, procedure, and practice provide that the program administrator is responsible for fiscal policy, management, and control. Management of fiscal operations may be delegated to a designated staff person.**

Comment:
The program administrator should have authority over fiscal matters in compliance with the general policies and practices of the governing body.

SELF-EVALUATION Agency Personnel	STANDARDS COMPLIANCE AUDIT Visiting Committee
Staff Signature(s): _____ _____ ❑ Compliance (list documentation) ❑ Noncompliance (see plan of action) ❑ Not applicable (justification attached) ❑ Plan of action waiver requested (justification attached) Prepare one of the following, as appropriate: 1) List documentation to support compliance; 2) Explain nonapplicability of standard: 3) Explain plan of action waiver request.	Auditor Signature(s): _____ _____ ❑ Compliance ❑ POA acceptable ❑ Noncompliance ❑ POA unacceptable ❑ Not Applicable ❑ Waiver acceptable ❑ Waiver unacceptable List deficiencies if standard is in noncompliance: **NOTE: List all deficiencies if standard is in noncompliance or not applicable. State exactly why standard is in noncompliance. Make complete comments in space above and attach any other information, if necessary. BE VERY SPECIFIC!**

1-EM-1B-02   **Written policy, procedure, and practice provide that the program has written fiscal policies and procedures adopted by the governing authority, including, at a minimum, the following: internal controls, petty cash, bonding, signature control on checks, offender funds, and employee expense reimbursements.**

Comment:
None.

SELF-EVALUATION Agency Personnel	STANDARDS COMPLIANCE AUDIT Visiting Committee
Staff Signature(s): _____ _____ ❑ Compliance (list documentation) ❑ Noncompliance (see plan of action) ❑ Not applicable (justification attached) ❑ Plan of action waiver requested (justification attached) Prepare one of the following, as appropriate: 1) List documentation to support compliance; 2) Explain nonapplicability of standard: 3) Explain plan of action waiver request.	Auditor Signature(s): _____ _____ ❑ Compliance ❑ POA acceptable ❑ Noncompliance ❑ POA unacceptable ❑ Not Applicable ❑ Waiver acceptable ❑ Waiver unacceptable List deficiencies if standard is in noncompliance: **NOTE: List all deficiencies if standard is in noncompliance or not applicable. State exactly why standard is in noncompliance. Make complete comments in space above and attach any other information, if necessary. BE VERY SPECIFIC!**

Budget Preparation

1-EM-1B-03   **Written policy, procedure, and practice provide that the program prepares an annual written budget of anticipated revenues and expenditures that is approved by the appropriate governing authority.**

Comment:
Before the beginning of the program's fiscal year, a budget of anticipated revenues and expenditures must be presented to and approved by the governing body.

SELF-EVALUATION Agency Personnel	STANDARDS COMPLIANCE AUDIT Visiting Committee
Staff Signature(s): _____ _____	Auditor Signature(s): _____ _____

<table>
<tr><td>

❑ Compliance (list documentation)
❑ Noncompliance (see plan of action)
❑ Not applicable (justification attached)
❑ Plan of action waiver requested (justification attached)

Prepare one of the following, as appropriate:

1) List documentation to support compliance;
2) Explain nonapplicability of standard:
3) Explain plan of action waiver request.

</td><td>

❑ Compliance   ❑ POA acceptable
❑ Noncompliance   ❑ POA unacceptable
❑ Not Applicable   ❑ Waiver acceptable
  ❑ Waiver unacceptable

List deficiencies if standard is in noncompliance:

NOTE: List all deficiencies if standard is in noncompliance or not applicable. State exactly why standard is in noncompliance. Make complete comments in space above and attach any other information, if necessary. BE VERY SPECIFIC!

</td></tr>
</table>

1-EM-1B-04   **Written policy, procedure, and practice provide that the program administrator participates in budget reviews conducted by the governing board or parent agency.**

Comment:
Because of the significance of budget reviews, the program administrator should participate in the process. In private agencies, the administrator would work directly with the governing authority. In public agencies, the administrator would work with the designated supervisory level within the parent agency.

SELF-EVALUATION Agency Personnel	STANDARDS COMPLIANCE AUDIT Visiting Committee
Staff Signature(s): _____ _____ ❑ Compliance (list documentation) ❑ Noncompliance (see plan of action) ❑ Not applicable (justification attached) ❑ Plan of action waiver requested (justification attached) Prepare one of the following, as appropriate: 1) List documentation to support compliance; 2) Explain nonapplicability of standard: 3) Explain plan of action waiver request.	Auditor Signature(s): _____ _____ ❑ Compliance ❑ POA acceptable ❑ Noncompliance ❑ POA unacceptable ❑ Not Applicable ❑ Waiver acceptable ❑ Waiver unacceptable List deficiencies if standard is in noncompliance: **NOTE: List all deficiencies if standard is in noncompliance or not applicable. State exactly why standard is in noncompliance. Make complete comments in space above and attach any other information, if necessary. BE VERY SPECIFIC!**

1-EM-1B-05   **Written policy, procedure, and practice govern revisions in the budget.**

Comment:
A fiscal budget serves as a guideline for anticipated revenues and expenditures that will periodically require revision.

SELF-EVALUATION Agency Personnel	STANDARDS COMPLIANCE AUDIT Visiting Committee
Staff Signature(s): _____ _____ ❑ Compliance (list documentation) ❑ Noncompliance (see plan of action) ❑ Not applicable (justification attached) ❑ Plan of action waiver requested (justification attached) Prepare one of the following, as appropriate: 1) List documentation to support compliance; 2) Explain nonapplicability of standard: 3) Explain plan of action waiver request.	Auditor Signature(s): _____ _____ ❑ Compliance ❑ POA acceptable ❑ Noncompliance ❑ POA unacceptable ❑ Not Applicable ❑ Waiver acceptable ❑ Waiver unacceptable List deficiencies if standard is in noncompliance: **NOTE: List all deficiencies if standard is in noncompliance or not applicable. State exactly why standard is in noncompliance. Make complete comments in space above and attach any other information, if necessary. BE VERY SPECIFIC!**

Cash Management

1-EM-1B-06   **Written policy, procedure, and practice provide that all monies collected in the program are placed daily in an officially designated and secure location.**

Comment:
None.

SELF-EVALUATION Agency Personnel	STANDARDS COMPLIANCE AUDIT Visiting Committee
Staff Signature(s): _____ _____ ❏ Compliance (list documentation) ❏ Noncompliance (see plan of action) ❏ Not applicable (justification attached) ❏ Plan of action waiver requested (justification attached) Prepare one of the following, as appropriate: 1) List documentation to support compliance; 2) Explain nonapplicability of standard: 3) Explain plan of action waiver request.	Auditor Signature(s): _____ _____ ❏ Compliance ❏ POA acceptable ❏ Noncompliance ❏ POA unacceptable ❏ Not Applicable ❏ Waiver acceptable ❏ Waiver unacceptable List deficiencies if standard is in noncompliance: **NOTE: List all deficiencies if standard is in noncompliance or not applicable. State exactly why standard is in noncompliance. Make complete comments in space above and attach any other information, if necessary. BE VERY SPECIFIC!**

1-EM-1B-07　**Written policy, procedure, and practice specify that the methods used for the receiving, safeguarding, disbursing, and recording of funds comply with accepted accounting procedures.**

Comment:
The agency's accounting procedures should minimize loss, mismanagement, and theft and should provide for "audit trails." The agency should be able to cite specific authoritative accounting sources as the basis for its written policies and procedures.

SELF-EVALUATION Agency Personnel	STANDARDS COMPLIANCE AUDIT Visiting Committee
Staff Signature(s): _____ _____	Auditor Signature(s): _____ _____

Self-Evaluation:

❏ Compliance (list documentation)
❏ Noncompliance (see plan of action)
❏ Not applicable (justification attached)
❏ Plan of action waiver requested (justification attached)

Prepare one of the following, as appropriate:

1) List documentation to support compliance;
2) Explain nonapplicability of standard:
3) Explain plan of action waiver request.

Standards Compliance Audit:

❏ Compliance　　❏ POA acceptable
❏ Noncompliance　❏ POA unacceptable
❏ Not Applicable　❏ Waiver acceptable
　　　　　　　　　❏ Waiver unacceptable

List deficiencies if standard is in noncompliance:

NOTE: List all deficiencies if standard is in noncompliance or not applicable. State exactly why standard is in noncompliance. Make complete comments in space above and attach any other information, if necessary. BE VERY SPECIFIC!

1-EM-1B-08   **Written policy, procedure, and practice provide that the program, at a minimum, prepares and distributes to its governing authority and appropriate agencies and individuals the following documents: income and expenditure statements, funding source financial reports, and independent audit reports.**

Comment:

The program must provide fiscal accountability reports. Current information is needed to meet objectives, prevent budget discrepancies, respond to emerging needs, and ensure that the flow of funds is proceeding as planned.

SELF-EVALUATION Agency Personnel	STANDARDS COMPLIANCE AUDIT Visiting Committee
Staff Signature(s): _____ _____ ❑ Compliance (list documentation) ❑ Noncompliance (see plan of action) ❑ Not applicable (justification attached) ❑ Plan of action waiver requested (justification attached) Prepare one of the following, as appropriate: 1) List documentation to support compliance; 2) Explain nonapplicability of standard: 3) Explain plan of action waiver request.	Auditor Signature(s): _____ _____ ❑ Compliance ❑ POA acceptable ❑ Noncompliance ❑ POA unacceptable ❑ Not Applicable ❑ Waiver acceptable ❑ Waiver unacceptable List deficiencies if standard is in noncompliance: **NOTE: List all deficiencies if standard is in noncompliance or not applicable. State exactly why standard is in noncompliance. Make complete comments in space above and attach any other information, if necessary. BE VERY SPECIFIC!**

Independent Audit

1-EM-1B-09   **Written policy, procedure, and practice provide for an independent financial audit of the program. This audit is conducted annually or as stipulated by statute or regulation, but at least every three years.**

Comment:
An outside, certified public accounting firm or a governmental auditing agency can conduct an audit and, by so doing, provide greater assurance to the program that its fiscal process is proficient and effective. The audit report also can provide the basis for correcting weakness in fiscal management and control.

SELF-EVALUATION Agency Personnel	STANDARDS COMPLIANCE AUDIT Visiting Committee
Staff Signature(s):	Auditor Signature(s):
_____	_____
_____	_____
❑ Compliance (list documentation) ❑ Noncompliance (see plan of action) ❑ Not applicable (justification attached) ❑ Plan of action waiver requested (justification attached)	❑ Compliance ❑ POA acceptable ❑ Noncompliance ❑ POA unacceptable ❑ Not Applicable ❑ Waiver acceptable ❑ Waiver unacceptable
Prepare one of the following, as appropriate: 1) List documentation to support compliance; 2) Explain nonapplicability of standard: 3) Explain plan of action waiver request.	List deficiencies if standard is in noncompliance: **NOTE: List all deficiencies if standard is in noncompliance or not applicable. State exactly why standard is in noncompliance. Make complete comments in space above and attach any other information, if necessary. BE VERY SPECIFIC!**

Purchasing/Inventory

1-EM-1B-10   **Written policy, procedure, and practice provide for purchasing and requisitioning of supplies and equipment and for property inventory and control.**

Comment:
Current and complete inventory records should be maintained for all property and equipment. Property records should include the following information: purchase date and price, source of funds, current value (if applicable), unit and location to which assigned, and name of person charged with custody.

SELF-EVALUATION Agency Personnel	STANDARDS COMPLIANCE AUDIT Visiting Committee
Staff Signature(s):	Auditor Signature(s):
_____ _____	_____ _____
❏ Compliance (list documentation) ❏ Noncompliance (see plan of action) ❏ Not applicable (justification attached) ❏ Plan of action waiver requested (justification attached) Prepare one of the following, as appropriate: 1) List documentation to support compliance; 2) Explain nonapplicability of standard: 3) Explain plan of action waiver request.	❏ Compliance ❏ POA acceptable ❏ Noncompliance ❏ POA unacceptable ❏ Not Applicable ❏ Waiver acceptable ❏ Waiver unacceptable List deficiencies if standard is in noncompliance: **NOTE: List all deficiencies if standard is in noncompliance or not applicable. State exactly why standard is in noncompliance. Make complete comments in space above and attach any other information, if necessary. BE VERY SPECIFIC!**

Program Insurance

1-EM-1B-11   **Written policy, procedure, and practice provide for insurance coverage that includes, at a minimum, property insurance and comprehensive general liability insurance; such insurance is provided either through private companies or self-insurance.**

Comment:
Comprehensive general liability coverage is the responsibility of the corporate entity or individual owner. It should include workers' compensation in accordance with the laws of the jurisdiction and insurance to protect employees against liability.

SELF-EVALUATION Agency Personnel	STANDARDS COMPLIANCE AUDIT Visiting Committee
Staff Signature(s):	Auditor Signature(s):
_____	_____
_____	_____
❑ Compliance (list documentation) ❑ Noncompliance (see plan of action) ❑ Not applicable (justification attached) ❑ Plan of action waiver requested (justification attached)	❑ Compliance ❑ POA acceptable ❑ Noncompliance ❑ POA unacceptable ❑ Not Applicable ❑ Waiver acceptable ❑ Waiver unacceptable
Prepare one of the following, as appropriate: 1) List documentation to support compliance; 2) Explain nonapplicability of standard: 3) Explain plan of action waiver request.	List deficiencies if standard is in noncompliance: **NOTE: List all deficiencies if standard is in noncompliance or not applicable. State exactly why standard is in noncompliance. Make complete comments in space above and attach any other information, if necessary. BE VERY SPECIFIC!**

Offender Funds/Payments

1-EM-1B-12   **Written policy, procedure, and practice provide that any financial transactions permitted between offenders, offenders and staff, or offenders and volunteers must be approved by the program administrator.**

Comment:
Uncontrolled financial transactions between offenders and offenders and staff can foster illegal activities.

SELF-EVALUATION Agency Personnel	STANDARDS COMPLIANCE AUDIT Visiting Committee
Staff Signature(s):	Auditor Signature(s):
_____ _____	_____ _____
❑ Compliance (list documentation) ❑ Noncompliance (see plan of action) ❑ Not applicable (justification attached) ❑ Plan of action waiver requested (justification attached) Prepare one of the following, as appropriate: 1) List documentation to support compliance; 2) Explain nonapplicability of standard: 3) Explain plan of action waiver request.	❑ Compliance ❑ POA acceptable ❑ Noncompliance ❑ POA unacceptable ❑ Not Applicable ❑ Waiver acceptable ❑ Waiver unacceptable List deficiencies if standard is in noncompliance: **NOTE: List all deficiencies if standard is in noncompliance or not applicable. State exactly why standard is in noncompliance. Make complete comments in space above and attach any other information, if necessary. BE VERY SPECIFIC!**

1-EM-1B-13   **Written policy, procedure, and practice provide that offenders pay for program services rendered at a reasonable rate as determined by the authority having jurisdiction.**

Comment:
None.

SELF-EVALUATION Agency Personnel	STANDARDS COMPLIANCE AUDIT Visiting Committee
Staff Signature(s): _____ _____ ❑ Compliance (list documentation) ❑ Noncompliance (see plan of action) ❑ Not applicable (justification attached) ❑ Plan of action waiver requested (justification attached) Prepare one of the following, as appropriate: 1) List documentation to support compliance; 2) Explain nonapplicability of standard: 3) Explain plan of action waiver request.	Auditor Signature(s): _____ _____ ❑ Compliance ❑ POA acceptable ❑ Noncompliance ❑ POA unacceptable ❑ Not Applicable ❑ Waiver acceptable ❑ Waiver unacceptable List deficiencies if standard is in noncompliance: **NOTE: List all deficiencies if standard is in noncompliance or not applicable. State exactly why standard is in noncompliance. Make complete comments in space above and attach any other information, if necessary. BE VERY SPECIFIC!**

1-EM-1B-14   **Written policy, procedure, and practice specify how the amount of the fee to the offender will be determined and when and how it will be collected and recorded. If the program is provided by a contractor, the contractor will provide the contracting agency, at least monthly, with an accounting of fees received, including the amount paid and the payer.**

Comment:
None.

SELF-EVALUATION Agency Personnel	STANDARDS COMPLIANCE AUDIT Visiting Committee
Staff Signature(s): _____ _____ ❏ Compliance (list documentation) ❏ Noncompliance (see plan of action) ❏ Not applicable (justification attached) ❏ Plan of action waiver requested (justification attached) Prepare one of the following, as appropriate: 1) List documentation to support compliance; 2) Explain nonapplicability of standard: 3) Explain plan of action waiver request.	Auditor Signature(s): _____ _____ ❏ Compliance ❏ POA acceptable ❏ Noncompliance ❏ POA unacceptable ❏ Not Applicable ❏ Waiver acceptable ❏ Waiver unacceptable List deficiencies if standard is in noncompliance: **NOTE: List all deficiencies if standard is in noncompliance or not applicable. State exactly why standard is in noncompliance. Make complete comments in space above and attach any other information, if necessary. BE VERY SPECIFIC!**

Section C
Personnel

Principle: A written body of policy and procedure provides the basis for human resource management.

Personnel Policy Manual

1-EM-1C-01   **Written policy, procedure, and practice provide that the program administrator reviews the program's internal personnel policies annually and submits to the parent agency any recommended changes.**

Comment:
None.

SELF-EVALUATION Agency Personnel	STANDARDS COMPLIANCE AUDIT Visiting Committee
Staff Signature(s): _____ _____ ❏ Compliance (list documentation) ❏ Noncompliance (see plan of action) ❏ Not applicable (justification attached) ❏ Plan of action waiver requested (justification attached) Prepare one of the following, as appropriate: 1) List documentation to support compliance; 2) Explain nonapplicability of standard; 3) Explain plan of action waiver request.	Auditor Signature(s): _____ _____ ❏ Compliance ❏ POA acceptable ❏ Noncompliance ❏ POA unacceptable ❏ Not Applicable ❏ Waiver acceptable ❏ Waiver unacceptable List deficiencies if standard is in noncompliance: **NOTE: List all deficiencies if standard is in noncompliance or not applicable. State exactly why standard is in noncompliance. Make complete comments in space above and attach any other information, if necessary. BE VERY SPECIFIC!**

1-EM-1C-02   Written policy, procedure, and practice provide that a personnel manual is available for employees that covers, at a minimum, the following areas:

- organizational chart
- staff development
- recruitment and selection
- promotion
- job qualifications and job descriptions
- affirmative action
- sexual harassment
- grievance and appeal procedures
- orientation
- employee evaluation
- personnel records
- benefits
- holidays
- leave
- hours of work
- probationary period
- compensation
- travel
- disciplinary procedures
- termination
- resignation

Comment:
The program's personnel policy should reflect its management philosophy and cover all areas relevant to the welfare of the personnel and program.

SELF-EVALUATION Agency Personnel	STANDARDS COMPLIANCE AUDIT Visiting Committee
Staff Signature(s):	Auditor Signature(s):
❑ Compliance (list documentation) ❑ Noncompliance (see plan of action) ❑ Not applicable (justification attached) ❑ Plan of action waiver requested (justification attached)	❑ Compliance ❑ POA acceptable ❑ Noncompliance ❑ POA unacceptable ❑ Not Applicable ❑ Waiver acceptable ❑ Waiver unacceptable
Prepare one of the following, as appropriate: 1) List documentation to support compliance; 2) Explain nonapplicability of standard: 3) Explain plan of action waiver request.	List deficiencies if standard is in noncompliance: **NOTE: List all deficiencies if standard is in noncompliance or not applicable. State exactly why standard is in noncompliance. Make complete comments in space above and attach any other information, if necessary. BE VERY SPECIFIC!**

1-EM-1C-03   **Written policy, procedure, and practice require employees to sign statements acknowledging access to and awareness of personnel policies and regulations.**

Comment:
None.

SELF-EVALUATION Agency Personnel	STANDARDS COMPLIANCE AUDIT Visiting Committee
Staff Signature(s): _____ _____ ❑ Compliance (list documentation) ❑ Noncompliance (see plan of action) ❑ Not applicable (justification attached) ❑ Plan of action waiver requested (justification attached) Prepare one of the following, as appropriate: 1) List documentation to support compliance; 2) Explain nonapplicability of standard: 3) Explain plan of action waiver request.	Auditor Signature(s): _____ _____ ❑ Compliance ❑ POA acceptable ❑ Noncompliance ❑ POA unacceptable ❑ Not Applicable ❑ Waiver acceptable ❑ Waiver unacceptable List deficiencies if standard is in noncompliance: **NOTE: List all deficiencies if standard is in noncompliance or not applicable. State exactly why standard is in noncompliance. Make complete comments in space above and attach any other information, if necessary. BE VERY SPECIFIC!**

Equal Employment Opportunity

1-EM-1C-04 **Written policy, procedure, and practice specify that equal employment opportunities exist for all positions. Personnel policies follow federal and state statutes regarding discrimination and exclusion from employment.**

Comment:
Equal employment opportunity is a public policy goal. All qualified persons should be able to compete equally for entry into and promotion from within the program. The affirmative action program should actively encourage the participation of members of minority groups, disabled persons, and women. The affirmative action program should include corrective actions, when needed, in policies regarding pay rate, demotion, transfer, layoff, termination, and promotion.

SELF-EVALUATION Agency Personnel	STANDARDS COMPLIANCE AUDIT Visiting Committee
Staff Signature(s):	Auditor Signature(s):
_____ _____	_____ _____
❑ Compliance (list documentation) ❑ Noncompliance (see plan of action) ❑ Not applicable (justification attached) ❑ Plan of action waiver requested (justification attached)	❑ Compliance ❑ POA acceptable ❑ Noncompliance ❑ POA unacceptable ❑ Not Applicable ❑ Waiver acceptable ❑ Waiver unacceptable
Prepare one of the following, as appropriate: 1) List documentation to support compliance; 2) Explain nonapplicability of standard: 3) Explain plan of action waiver request.	List deficiencies if standard is in noncompliance: NOTE: List all deficiencies if standard is in noncompliance or not applicable. State exactly why standard is in noncompliance. Make complete comments in space above and attach any other information, if necessary. BE VERY SPECIFIC!

Sexual Harassment

1-EM-1C-05   **Written policy, procedure, and practice prohibit sexual harassment.**

Comment:
Program administrators should have as their objective the creation of a workplace that is free from all forms of discrimination, including sexual harassment. Program policy clearly indicates that sexual harassment, either explicit or implicit, is strictly prohibited. Employees, offenders, and agents of the program, including volunteers, contractors, and vendors, must be advised that they are subject to disciplinary action, including dismissal and termination of contracts and/or services, if found guilty of sexual harassment charges brought by employees or offenders.

SELF-EVALUATION Agency Personnel	STANDARDS COMPLIANCE AUDIT Visiting Committee
Staff Signature(s): _____ _____ ❑ Compliance (list documentation) ❑ Noncompliance (see plan of action) ❑ Not applicable (justification attached) ❑ Plan of action waiver requested (justification attached) Prepare one of the following, as appropriate: 1) List documentation to support compliance; 2) Explain nonapplicability of standard: 3) Explain plan of action waiver request.	Auditor Signature(s): _____ _____ ❑ Compliance ❑ POA acceptable ❑ Noncompliance ❑ POA unacceptable ❑ Not Applicable ❑ Waiver acceptable ❑ Waiver unacceptable List deficiencies if standard is in noncompliance: **NOTE: List all deficiencies if standard is in noncompliance or not applicable. State exactly why standard is in noncompliance. Make complete comments in space above and attach any other information, if necessary. BE VERY SPECIFIC!**

Drug-free Workplace

1-EM-1C-06   **Written policy, procedure, and practice specify support for a drug-free workplace for all employees. This policy, which is reviewed annually, includes, at a minimum, the following:**

- **prohibition of the use of illegal drugs**
- **prohibition of possession of any illegal drug, except in the performance of official duties**
- **procedures to be used to ensure compliance**
- **opportunities available for treatment and/or counseling for drug abuse**
- **penalties for violation of the policy**

Comment:
None.

SELF-EVALUATION Agency Personnel	STANDARDS COMPLIANCE AUDIT Visiting Committee
Staff Signature(s):	Auditor Signature(s):

Self-Evaluation — Agency Personnel:

❏ Compliance (list documentation)
❏ Noncompliance (see plan of action)
❏ Not applicable (justification attached)
❏ Plan of action waiver requested (justification attached)

Prepare one of the following, as appropriate:

1) List documentation to support compliance;
2) Explain nonapplicability of standard:
3) Explain plan of action waiver request.

Standards Compliance Audit — Visiting Committee:

❏ Compliance   ❏ POA acceptable
❏ Noncompliance   ❏ POA unacceptable
❏ Not Applicable   ❏ Waiver acceptable
                 ❏ Waiver unacceptable

List deficiencies if standard is in noncompliance:

NOTE: List all deficiencies if standard is in noncompliance or not applicable. State exactly why standard is in noncompliance. Make complete comments in space above and attach any other information, if necessary. BE VERY SPECIFIC!

Job Descriptions

1-EM-1C-07 **Written policy, procedure, and practice provide that there are written job descriptions and job qualifications for all positions. Each job description includes, at a minimum: job title, responsibilities of the position, required minimum experience, and education.**

Comment:
The job description can be a useful tool in evaluating employee performance. It also can provide the employee with clarification of the duties and responsibilities of the position.

SELF-EVALUATION Agency Personnel	STANDARDS COMPLIANCE AUDIT Visiting Committee
Staff Signature(s): _____ _____ ❑ Compliance (list documentation) ❑ Noncompliance (see plan of action) ❑ Not applicable (justification attached) ❑ Plan of action waiver requested (justification attached) Prepare one of the following, as appropriate: 1) List documentation to support compliance; 2) Explain nonapplicability of standard: 3) Explain plan of action waiver request.	Auditor Signature(s): _____ ❑ Compliance ❑ POA acceptable ❑ Noncompliance ❑ POA unacceptable ❑ Not Applicable ❑ Waiver acceptable ❑ Waiver unacceptable List deficiencies if standard is in noncompliance: **NOTE: List all deficiencies if standard is in noncompliance or not applicable. State exactly why standard is in noncompliance. Make complete comments in space above and attach any other information, if necessary. BE VERY SPECIFIC!**

Compensation and Benefits

1-EM-1C-08   **Written policy, procedure, and practice provide that compensation and benefit levels for all personnel are comparable to similar occupational groups in the community.**

Comment:
Competitive salaries and benefits are necessary for the recruitment and retention of high-caliber staff.

SELF-EVALUATION Agency Personnel	STANDARDS COMPLIANCE AUDIT Visiting Committee
Staff Signature(s): _____ _____	Auditor Signature(s): _____ _____

<table>
<tr>
<td>

❏ Compliance (list documentation)
❏ Noncompliance (see plan of action)
❏ Not applicable (justification attached)
❏ Plan of action waiver requested (justification attached)

Prepare one of the following, as appropriate:

1) List documentation to support compliance;
2) Explain nonapplicability of standard:
3) Explain plan of action waiver request.

</td>
<td>

❏ Compliance   ❏ POA acceptable
❏ Noncompliance   ❏ POA unacceptable
❏ Not Applicable   ❏ Waiver acceptable
                         ❏ Waiver unacceptable

List deficiencies if standard is in noncompliance:

NOTE: List all deficiencies if standard is in noncompliance or not applicable. State exactly why standard is in noncompliance. Make complete comments in space above and attach any other information, if necessary. BE VERY SPECIFIC!

</td>
</tr>
</table>

Criminal Record Check

1-EM-1C-09   **Written policy, procedure, and practice provide that criminal record checks are conducted on all new employees and volunteers in accordance with state and federal statutes.**

Comment:
The program administrator should know of any criminal conviction that could directly affect an employee's job performance.

SELF-EVALUATION Agency Personnel	STANDARDS COMPLIANCE AUDIT Visiting Committee
Staff Signature(s): _____ _____	Auditor Signature(s): _____ _____

SELF-EVALUATION (Agency Personnel)

❑ Compliance (list documentation)
❑ Noncompliance (see plan of action)
❑ Not applicable (justification attached)
❑ Plan of action waiver requested (justification attached)

Prepare one of the following, as appropriate:

1) List documentation to support compliance;
2) Explain nonapplicability of standard:
3) Explain plan of action waiver request.

STANDARDS COMPLIANCE AUDIT (Visiting Committee)

❑ Compliance   ❑ POA acceptable
❑ Noncompliance   ❑ POA unacceptable
❑ Not Applicable   ❑ Waiver acceptable
                      ❑ Waiver unacceptable

List deficiencies if standard is in noncompliance:

NOTE: List all deficiencies if standard is in noncompliance or not applicable. State exactly why standard is in noncompliance. Make complete comments in space above and attach any other information, if necessary. BE VERY SPECIFIC!

Termination/Demotion

1-EM-1C-10   **Written policy, procedure, and practice provide that termination or demotion is permitted only for a good cause and, if requested, subsequent to a formal hearing on specific charges.**

Comment:
None.

SELF-EVALUATION Agency Personnel	STANDARDS COMPLIANCE AUDIT Visiting Committee
Staff Signature(s): _____ _____ ❑ Compliance (list documentation) ❑ Noncompliance (see plan of action) ❑ Not applicable (justification attached) ❑ Plan of action waiver requested (justification attached) Prepare one of the following, as appropriate: 1) List documentation to support compliance; 2) Explain nonapplicability of standard: 3) Explain plan of action waiver request.	Auditor Signature(s): _____ _____ ❑ Compliance ❑ POA acceptable ❑ Noncompliance ❑ POA unacceptable ❑ Not Applicable ❑ Waiver acceptable ❑ Waiver unacceptable List deficiencies if standard is in noncompliance: **NOTE: List all deficiencies if standard is in noncompliance or not applicable. State exactly why standard is in noncompliance. Make complete comments in space above and attach any other information, if necessary. BE VERY SPECIFIC!**

Personnel Records

1-EM-1C-11 **Written policy, procedure, and practice provide for a confidential personnel record for each employee.**

Comment:
The personnel record should contain the following: initial applications, reference letters, results of employee investigation, verification of training and experience, wage and salary information, job performance evaluations, incident reports if any, and commendations and disciplinary actions, if any.

SELF-EVALUATION Agency Personnel	STANDARDS COMPLIANCE AUDIT Visiting Committee
Staff Signature(s):	Auditor Signature(s):
_____ _____	_____ _____
❑ Compliance (list documentation) ❑ Noncompliance (see plan of action) ❑ Not applicable (justification attached) ❑ Plan of action waiver requested (justification attached) Prepare one of the following, as appropriate: 1) List documentation to support compliance; 2) Explain nonapplicability of standard; 3) Explain plan of action waiver request.	❑ Compliance ❑ POA acceptable ❑ Noncompliance ❑ POA unacceptable ❑ Not Applicable ❑ Waiver acceptable ❑ Waiver unacceptable List deficiencies if standard is in noncompliance: **NOTE: List all deficiencies if standard is in noncompliance or not applicable. State exactly why standard is in noncompliance. Make complete comments in space above and attach any other information, if necessary. BE VERY SPECIFIC!**

1-EM-1C-12 **Written policy, procedure, and practice provide that employees may challenge information in their personnel file. The information may be corrected or removed, if proved inaccurate.**

Comment:

Employees should be allowed to review their personnel file to ensure that it is current and accurate. Written procedure should specify the means for correcting discrepancies.

SELF-EVALUATION Agency Personnel	STANDARDS COMPLIANCE AUDIT Visiting Committee
Staff Signature(s):	Auditor Signature(s):
 _____ _____	 _____ _____
❑ Compliance (list documentation) ❑ Noncompliance (see plan of action) ❑ Not applicable (justification attached) ❑ Plan of action waiver requested (justification attached) Prepare one of the following, as appropriate: 1) List documentation to support compliance; 2) Explain nonapplicability of standard: 3) Explain plan of action waiver request.	❑ Compliance ❑ POA acceptable ❑ Noncompliance ❑ POA unacceptable ❑ Not Applicable ❑ Waiver acceptable ❑ Waiver unacceptable List deficiencies if standard is in noncompliance: **NOTE: List all deficiencies if standard is in noncompliance or not applicable. State exactly why standard is in noncompliance. Make complete comments in space above and attach any other information, if necessary. BE VERY SPECIFIC!**

1-EM-1C-13 **Written policy, procedure, and practice provide for an annual written performance review of each employee. The review is based on defined criteria, and the results are discussed with the employee. The review is signed by the employee and the evaluator.**

Comment:
Performance reviews should be an ongoing process with written evaluations completed at least annually. They should be objective and based on specific job criteria and explicit performance standards.

SELF-EVALUATION Agency Personnel	STANDARDS COMPLIANCE AUDIT Visiting Committee
Staff Signature(s): _____ _____	Auditor Signature(s): _____ _____

Self-Evaluation:

❑ Compliance (list documentation)
❑ Noncompliance (see plan of action)
❑ Not applicable (justification attached)
❑ Plan of action waiver requested (justification attached)

Prepare one of the following, as appropriate:

1) List documentation to support compliance;
2) Explain nonapplicability of standard:
3) Explain plan of action waiver request.

Standards Compliance Audit:

❑ Compliance   ❑ POA acceptable
❑ Noncompliance   ❑ POA unacceptable
❑ Not Applicable   ❑ Waiver acceptable
                      ❑ Waiver unacceptable

List deficiencies if standard is in noncompliance:

NOTE: List all deficiencies if standard is in noncompliance or not applicable. State exactly why standard is in noncompliance. Make complete comments in space above and attach any other information, if necessary. BE VERY SPECIFIC!

Confidentiality of Information

1-EM-1C-14   **Written policy, procedure, and practice provide that employees, consultants, volunteers, and contract personnel are informed in writing about the program's policies on confidentiality of information and agree in writing to abide by them.**

Comment:
The written policies should specify what types of information are confidential between worker and offender, what types may be shared with other program personnel, and what types can be communicated to persons outside the program.

SELF-EVALUATION Agency Personnel	STANDARDS COMPLIANCE AUDIT Visiting Committee
Staff Signature(s): _____ _____ ❑ Compliance (list documentation) ❑ Noncompliance (see plan of action) ❑ Not applicable (justification attached) ❑ Plan of action waiver requested (justification attached) Prepare one of the following, as appropriate: 1) List documentation to support compliance; 2) Explain nonapplicability of standard: 3) Explain plan of action waiver request.	Auditor Signature(s): _____ _____ ❑ Compliance ❑ POA acceptable ❑ Noncompliance ❑ POA unacceptable ❑ Not Applicable ❑ Waiver acceptable ❑ Waiver unacceptable List deficiencies if standard is in noncompliance: **NOTE: List all deficiencies if standard is in noncompliance or not applicable. State exactly why standard is in noncompliance. Make complete comments in space above and attach any other information, if necessary. BE VERY SPECIFIC!**

Staffing Requirements

1-EM-1C-15   **Written policy, procedure, and practice provide that the program administrator and/or governing authority systematically determine and review staffing requirements at least annually.**

Comment:
In order to provide clients access to staff and available services, determination of staff requirements should reflect factors such as legal requirements, goals to be accomplished, character and needs of clients, and other duties required of staff.

SELF-EVALUATION Agency Personnel	STANDARDS COMPLIANCE AUDIT Visiting Committee
Staff Signature(s): _____ _____ ❑ Compliance (list documentation) ❑ Noncompliance (see plan of action) ❑ Not applicable (justification attached) ❑ Plan of action waiver requested (justification attached) Prepare one of the following, as appropriate: 1) List documentation to support compliance; 2) Explain nonapplicability of standard: 3) Explain plan of action waiver request.	Auditor Signature(s): _____ _____ ❑ Compliance ❑ POA acceptable ❑ Noncompliance ❑ POA unacceptable ❑ Not Applicable ❑ Waiver acceptable ❑ Waiver unacceptable List deficiencies if standard is in noncompliance: **NOTE: List all deficiencies if standard is in noncompliance or not applicable. State exactly why standard is in noncompliance. Make complete comments in space above and attach any other information, if necessary. BE VERY SPECIFIC!**

1-EM-1C-16   **Written policy, procedure, and practice provide for a staffing plan that provides essential services during regular days off, vacation, sick leave, and emergencies.**

Comment:
None.

SELF-EVALUATION Agency Personnel	STANDARDS COMPLIANCE AUDIT Visiting Committee
Staff Signature(s):	Auditor Signature(s):
❑ Compliance (list documentation) ❑ Noncompliance (see plan of action) ❑ Not applicable (justification attached) ❑ Plan of action waiver requested (justification attached) Prepare one of the following, as appropriate: 1) List documentation to support compliance; 2) Explain nonapplicability of standard: 3) Explain plan of action waiver request.	❑ Compliance ❑ POA acceptable ❑ Noncompliance ❑ POA unacceptable ❑ Not Applicable ❑ Waiver acceptable ❑ Waiver unacceptable List deficiencies if standard is in noncompliance: **NOTE: List all deficiencies if standard is in noncompliance or not applicable. State exactly why standard is in noncompliance. Make complete comments in space above and attach any other information, if necessary. BE VERY SPECIFIC!**

Grievance Procedures

1-EM-1C-17 **Written policy, procedure, and practice provide that there is an employee grievance procedure.**

Comment:
The agency grievance procedure should clearly specify the process to be followed by the employee when a grievance exists, and should identify, at a minimum: the hearing body, the manner in which a grievance is presented, and provisions for appeal. The written grievance procedure should be distributed and explained to all new employees.

SELF-EVALUATION Agency Personnel	STANDARDS COMPLIANCE AUDIT Visiting Committee
Staff Signature(s): _____ _____	Auditor Signature(s): _____ _____
❑ Compliance (list documentation) ❑ Noncompliance (see plan of action) ❑ Not applicable (justification attached) ❑ Plan of action waiver requested (justification attached) Prepare one of the following, as appropriate: 1) List documentation to support compliance; 2) Explain nonapplicability of standard: 3) Explain plan of action waiver request.	❑ Compliance ❑ POA acceptable ❑ Noncompliance ❑ POA unacceptable ❑ Not Applicable ❑ Waiver acceptable ❑ Waiver unacceptable List deficiencies if standard is in noncompliance: NOTE: List all deficiencies if standard is in noncompliance or not applicable. State exactly why standard is in noncompliance. Make complete comments in space above and attach any other information, if necessary. BE VERY SPECIFIC!

1-EM-1C-18   Written policy, procedure, and practice provide for effective employee/management relations.

Comment:
The agency can operate more effectively with specific procedures for the recognition and resolution of legitimate employee concerns. This system may include, but not be limited to: steps for resolving grievances and adverse actions, an appeals procedure, scheduled meetings between employee groups and the agency, and written records of meetings between employee groups and the agency.

SELF-EVALUATION Agency Personnel	STANDARDS COMPLIANCE AUDIT Visiting Committee
Staff Signature(s):	Auditor Signature(s):

SELF-EVALUATION

Staff Signature(s):

_____

_____

❏ Compliance (list documentation)
❏ Noncompliance (see plan of action)
❏ Not applicable (justification attached)
❏ Plan of action waiver requested (justification attached)

Prepare one of the following, as appropriate:

1) List documentation to support compliance;
2) Explain nonapplicability of standard:
3) Explain plan of action waiver request.

STANDARDS COMPLIANCE AUDIT

Auditor Signature(s):

_____

_____

❏ Compliance   ❏ POA acceptable
❏ Noncompliance   ❏ POA unacceptable
❏ Not Applicable   ❏ Waiver acceptable
                    ❏ Waiver unacceptable

List deficiencies if standard is in noncompliance:

NOTE: List all deficiencies if standard is in noncompliance or not applicable. State exactly why standard is in noncompliance. Make complete comments in space above and attach any other information, if necessary. BE VERY SPECIFIC!

Code of Ethics

1-EM-1C-19   **There is a written code of ethics prohibiting employees from using their positions for personal gain and from engaging in activities that constitute a conflict of interest. The code of ethics is given to all employees at their orientation and is reviewed as a part of annual training.**

Comment:
None.

SELF-EVALUATION Agency Personnel	STANDARDS COMPLIANCE AUDIT Visiting Committee
Staff Signature(s): _____ _____ ❑ Compliance (list documentation) ❑ Noncompliance (see plan of action) ❑ Not applicable (justification attached) ❑ Plan of action waiver requested (justification attached) Prepare one of the following, as appropriate: 1) List documentation to support compliance; 2) Explain nonapplicability of standard: 3) Explain plan of action waiver request.	Auditor Signature(s): _____ _____ ❑ Compliance ❑ POA acceptable ❑ Noncompliance ❑ POA unacceptable ❑ Not Applicable ❑ Waiver acceptable ❑ Waiver unacceptable List deficiencies if standard is in noncompliance: **NOTE: List all deficiencies if standard is in noncompliance or not applicable. State exactly why standard is in noncompliance. Make complete comments in space above and attach any other information, if necessary. BE VERY SPECIFIC!**

Section D
Training and Staff Development

Principle: A written body of policy and procedure establishes the program's training and staff development programs, including training requirements for all categories of personnel.

Program Coordination and Supervision

1-EM-1D-01   **Written policy, procedure, and practice provide that the staff development and training program is planned, coordinated, and supervised by a qualified employee. The training plan is reviewed annually.**

Comment:
None.

SELF-EVALUATION Agency Personnel	STANDARDS COMPLIANCE AUDIT Visiting Committee
Staff Signature(s): _____ _____ ❑ Compliance (list documentation) ❑ Noncompliance (see plan of action) ❑ Not applicable (justification attached) ❑ Plan of action waiver requested (justification attached) Prepare one of the following, as appropriate: 1) List documentation to support compliance; 2) Explain nonapplicability of standard: 3) Explain plan of action waiver request.	Auditor Signature(s): _____ _____ ❑ Compliance ❑ POA acceptable ❑ Noncompliance ❑ POA unacceptable ❑ Not Applicable ❑ Waiver acceptable ❑ Waiver unacceptable List deficiencies if standard is in noncompliance: **NOTE: List all deficiencies if standard is in noncompliance or not applicable. State exactly why standard is in noncompliance. Make complete comments in space above and attach any other information, if necessary. BE VERY SPECIFIC!**

1-EM-1D-02   **Written policy, procedure, and practice provide that the training plan is developed, evaluated, and updated at least quarterly to determine progress and to resolve problems. A written record of the review is signed and maintained.**

Comment:
Training should be responsive to position requirements, professional development needs, current issues, and new theories, techniques, and technologies. The needs assessment may require information from many sources: observation and analysis of job components, staff surveys regarding training needs, reviews of program operations, staff reports, and evaluations and findings from sources within and outside the jurisdiction.

SELF-EVALUATION Agency Personnel	STANDARDS COMPLIANCE AUDIT Visiting Committee
Staff Signature(s):	Auditor Signature(s):
_____ _____	_____ _____
❑ Compliance (list documentation) ❑ Noncompliance (see plan of action) ❑ Not applicable (justification attached) ❑ Plan of action waiver requested (justification attached)	❑ Compliance ❑ POA acceptable ❑ Noncompliance ❑ POA unacceptable ❑ Not Applicable ❑ Waiver acceptable ❑ Waiver unacceptable
Prepare one of the following, as appropriate: 1) List documentation to support compliance; 2) Explain nonapplicability of standard: 3) Explain plan of action waiver request.	List deficiencies if standard is in noncompliance: **NOTE: List all deficiencies if standard is in noncompliance or not applicable. State exactly why standard is in noncompliance. Make complete comments in space above and attach any other information, if necessary. BE VERY SPECIFIC!**

Training Evaluation

1-EM-1D-03   **Written policy, procedure, and practice provide for ongoing written evaluations of all pre-service, in-service, and specialized training programs.**

Comment:
Ongoing evaluations should include appraisals from trainees and supervisors.

SELF-EVALUATION Agency Personnel	STANDARDS COMPLIANCE AUDIT Visiting Committee
Staff Signature(s): _____ _____ ❏ Compliance (list documentation) ❏ Noncompliance (see plan of action) ❏ Not applicable (justification attached) ❏ Plan of action waiver requested (justification attached) Prepare one of the following, as appropriate: 1) List documentation to support compliance; 2) Explain nonapplicability of standard: 3) Explain plan of action waiver request.	Auditor Signature(s): _____ _____ ❏ Compliance ❏ POA acceptable ❏ Noncompliance ❏ POA unacceptable ❏ Not Applicable ❏ Waiver acceptable ❏ Waiver unacceptable List deficiencies if standard is in noncompliance: **NOTE: List all deficiencies if standard is in noncompliance or not applicable. State exactly why standard is in noncompliance. Make complete comments in space above and attach any other information, if necessary. BE VERY SPECIFIC!**

Training Resources

1-EM-1D-04   **Written policy, procedure, and practice provide that the program's training and staff development program uses community resources.**

Comment:
Electronic monitoring agencies should seek the guidance and assistance of many types of agencies in connection with administering their training programs. College and university faculty may be of assistance in developing training courses and curricula and in formulating techniques for evaluating the staff development program. The National Institute of Corrections, state and local employment and training agencies, military establishments, large corporations, and libraries are all examples of community resources that can be used for assistance, materials, and equipment.

SELF-EVALUATION Agency Personnel	STANDARDS COMPLIANCE AUDIT Visiting Committee
Staff Signature(s):	Auditor Signature(s):
❏ Compliance (list documentation) ❏ Noncompliance (see plan of action) ❏ Not applicable (justification attached) ❏ Plan of action waiver requested (justification attached) Prepare one of the following, as appropriate: 1) List documentation to support compliance; 2) Explain nonapplicability of standard: 3) Explain plan of action waiver request.	❏ Compliance ❏ POA acceptable ❏ Noncompliance ❏ POA unacceptable ❏ Not Applicable ❏ Waiver acceptable ❏ Waiver unacceptable List deficiencies if standard is in noncompliance: **NOTE: List all deficiencies if standard is in noncompliance or not applicable. State exactly why standard is in noncompliance. Make complete comments in space above and attach any other information, if necessary. BE VERY SPECIFIC!**

1-EM-1D-05   **Written policy, procedure, and practice provide that all training programs are presented by persons who are qualified in the areas in which they conduct training.**

Comment:
None.

SELF-EVALUATION Agency Personnel	STANDARDS COMPLIANCE AUDIT Visiting Committee
Staff Signature(s): _____ _____ ❑ Compliance (list documentation) ❑ Noncompliance (see plan of action) ❑ Not applicable (justification attached) ❑ Plan of action waiver requested (justification attached) Prepare one of the following, as appropriate: 1) List documentation to support compliance; 2) Explain nonapplicability of standard: 3) Explain plan of action waiver request.	Auditor Signature(s): _____ _____ ❑ Compliance ❑ POA acceptable ❑ Noncompliance ❑ POA unacceptable ❑ Not Applicable ❑ Waiver acceptable ❑ Waiver unacceptable List deficiencies if standard is in noncompliance: **NOTE: List all deficiencies if standard is in noncompliance or not applicable. State exactly why standard is in noncompliance. Make complete comments in space above and attach any other information, if necessary. BE VERY SPECIFIC!**

Reference Services

1-EM-1D-06   **Written policy, procedure, and practice provide that library and reference services are available to complement the training and staff development program.**

Comment:

Reference materials should be accessible to employees. Materials not usually available at the program should be acquired through other sources, such as clearinghouses and interlibrary loans.

SELF-EVALUATION Agency Personnel	STANDARDS COMPLIANCE AUDIT Visiting Committee
Staff Signature(s): _____ _____	Auditor Signature(s): _____ _____

Staff Signature(s):

_____

_____

❑ Compliance (list documentation)
❑ Noncompliance (see plan of action)
❑ Not applicable (justification attached)
❑ Plan of action waiver requested (justification attached)

Prepare one of the following, as appropriate:

1) List documentation to support compliance;
2) Explain nonapplicability of standard:
3) Explain plan of action waiver request.

Auditor Signature(s):

_____

_____

❑ Compliance   ❑ POA acceptable
❑ Noncompliance   ❑ POA unacceptable
❑ Not Applicable   ❑ Waiver acceptable
                      ❑ Waiver unacceptable

List deficiencies if standard is in noncompliance:

NOTE: List all deficiencies if standard is in noncompliance or not applicable. State exactly why standard is in noncompliance. Make complete comments in space above and attach any other information, if necessary. BE VERY SPECIFIC!

Space and Equipment

1-EM-1D-07   **Written policy, procedure, and practice provide that space and equipment required for training and staff development programs are available.**

Comment:
None.

SELF-EVALUATION Agency Personnel	STANDARDS COMPLIANCE AUDIT Visiting Committee
Staff Signature(s):	Auditor Signature(s):

Staff Signature(s):

_____

_____

❑ Compliance (list documentation)
❑ Noncompliance (see plan of action)
❑ Not applicable (justification attached)
❑ Plan of action waiver requested (justification attached)

Prepare one of the following, as appropriate:

1) List documentation to support compliance;
2) Explain nonapplicability of standard:
3) Explain plan of action waiver request.

Auditor Signature(s):

_____

_____

❑ Compliance   ❑ POA acceptable
❑ Noncompliance   ❑ POA unacceptable
❑ Not Applicable   ❑ Waiver acceptable
                            ❑ Waiver unacceptable

List deficiencies if standard is in noncompliance:

NOTE: List all deficiencies if standard is in noncompliance or not applicable. State exactly why standard is in noncompliance. Make complete comments in space above and attach any other information, if necessary. BE VERY SPECIFIC!

Orientation Training

1-EM-1D-08   **Written policy, procedure, and practice provide that all new employees receive 40 hours of orientation training before undertaking their assignments. Orientation training includes, at a minimum, the following: a historical perspective of the program, program goals and objectives, program rules and regulations, job responsibilities, personnel policies, offender supervision, and report preparation. Each employee signs and dates a statement indicating that orientation has been received.**

Comment:
Supervisory personnel should provide orientation for all newly employed personnel to familiarize them with program policies and procedures.

SELF-EVALUATION Agency Personnel	STANDARDS COMPLIANCE AUDIT Visiting Committee
Staff Signature(s): _____ _____ ❑ Compliance (list documentation) ❑ Noncompliance (see plan of action) ❑ Not applicable (justification attached) ❑ Plan of action waiver requested (justification attached) Prepare one of the following, as appropriate: 1) List documentation to support compliance; 2) Explain nonapplicability of standard: 3) Explain plan of action waiver request.	Auditor Signature(s): _____ _____ ❑ Compliance ❑ POA acceptable ❑ Noncompliance ❑ POA unacceptable ❑ Not Applicable ❑ Waiver acceptable ❑ Waiver unacceptable List deficiencies if standard is in noncompliance: **NOTE: List all deficiencies if standard is in noncompliance or not applicable. State exactly why standard is in noncompliance. Make complete comments in space above and attach any other information, if necessary. BE VERY SPECIFIC!**

Personnel Training

1-EM-1D-09   **Written policy, procedure, and practice provide that all administrative, managerial and professional specialist staff receive 40 hours of training in addition to orientation training during the first year of employment and 40 hours of training each year thereafter. At a minimum, this training covers the following areas: general management, legal responsibilities, legal restrictions, labor law, employee-management relations, the criminal justice system, and relationships with other agencies.**

Comment:
None.

SELF-EVALUATION Agency Personnel	STANDARDS COMPLIANCE AUDIT Visiting Committee
Staff Signature(s):	Auditor Signature(s):

SELF-EVALUATION — Agency Personnel

☐ Compliance (list documentation)
☐ Noncompliance (see plan of action)
☐ Not applicable (justification attached)
☐ Plan of action waiver requested (justification attached)

Prepare one of the following, as appropriate:

1) List documentation to support compliance;
2) Explain nonapplicability of standard:
3) Explain plan of action waiver request.

STANDARDS COMPLIANCE AUDIT — Visiting Committee

☐ Compliance   ☐ POA acceptable
☐ Noncompliance   ☐ POA unacceptable
☐ Not Applicable   ☐ Waiver acceptable
                   ☐ Waiver unacceptable

List deficiencies if standard is in noncompliance:

NOTE: List all deficiencies if standard is in noncompliance or not applicable. State exactly why standard is in noncompliance. Make complete comments in space above and attach any other information, if necessary. BE VERY SPECIFIC!

1-EM-1D-10 **Written policy, procedure, and practice provide that all employees who have regular or daily contact with offenders receive 40 hours of training in addition to orientation training during their first year of employment and 40 hours of training each year thereafter.**

Comment:
Personnel whose work requires contact with offenders in person or by telephone should receive basic training in offender supervision and security as well as specialized training in their field. These individuals should be familiar with policies and procedures of the facility, plus the basic rules of offender supervision and security. Ongoing training during subsequent years of employment enables employees to sharpen skills and keep abreast of changes in operational procedures.

SELF-EVALUATION Agency Personnel	STANDARDS COMPLIANCE AUDIT Visiting Committee
Staff Signature(s):	Auditor Signature(s):
❑ Compliance (list documentation) ❑ Noncompliance (see plan of action) ❑ Not applicable (justification attached) ❑ Plan of action waiver requested (justification attached)	❑ Compliance ❑ POA acceptable ❑ Noncompliance ❑ POA unacceptable ❑ Not Applicable ❑ Waiver acceptable ❑ Waiver unacceptable
Prepare one of the following, as appropriate: 1) List documentation to support compliance; 2) Explain nonapplicability of standard: 3) Explain plan of action waiver request.	List deficiencies if standard is in noncompliance: NOTE: List all deficiencies if standard is in noncompliance or not applicable. State exactly why standard is in noncompliance. Make complete comments in space above and attach any other information, if necessary. BE VERY SPECIFIC!

1-EM-1D-11   **Written policy, procedure, and practice provide that all employees who have minimal or no contact with offenders receive an additional 16 hours of training during the first year of employment and 16 hours of training each year thereafter.**

Comment:
Personnel who are not in continuous contact with offenders should be given orientation to the policies, organization, structure, programs, and regulations of the program and parent agency, as well as task orientation relative to their particular job assignments.

SELF-EVALUATION Agency Personnel	STANDARDS COMPLIANCE AUDIT Visiting Committee

Staff Signature(s):

_____

_____

❏ Compliance (list documentation)
❏ Noncompliance (see plan of action)
❏ Not applicable (justification attached)
❏ Plan of action waiver requested (justification attached)

Prepare one of the following, as appropriate:

1) List documentation to support compliance;
2) Explain nonapplicability of standard:
3) Explain plan of action waiver request.

Auditor Signature(s):

_____

_____

❏ Compliance   ❏ POA acceptable
❏ Noncompliance   ❏ POA unacceptable
❏ Not Applicable   ❏ Waiver acceptable
                              ❏ Waiver unacceptable

List deficiencies if standard is in noncompliance:

NOTE: List all deficiencies if standard is in noncompliance or not applicable. State exactly why standard is in noncompliance. Make complete comments in space above and attach any other information, if necessary. BE VERY SPECIFIC!

Part-time Staff/Volunteers

1-EM-1D-12 **All part-time staff, volunteers, and contract personnel receive orientation appropriate to their assignments and additional training, as needed.**

Comment:
Part-time staff, volunteers, and contract personnel should receive orientation to program rules, security, and operational procedures.

SELF-EVALUATION Agency Personnel	STANDARDS COMPLIANCE AUDIT Visiting Committee
Staff Signature(s): _____ _____ ❑ Compliance (list documentation) ❑ Noncompliance (see plan of action) ❑ Not applicable (justification attached) ❑ Plan of action waiver requested (justification attached) Prepare one of the following, as appropriate: 1) List documentation to support compliance; 2) Explain nonapplicability of standard: 3) Explain plan of action waiver request.	Auditor Signature(s): _____ _____ ❑ Compliance ❑ POA acceptable ❑ Noncompliance ❑ POA unacceptable ❑ Not Applicable ❑ Waiver acceptable ❑ Waiver unacceptable List deficiencies if standard is in noncompliance: **NOTE: List all deficiencies if standard is in noncompliance or not applicable. State exactly why standard is in noncompliance. Make complete comments in space above and attach any other information, if necessary. BE VERY SPECIFIC!**

Continuing Education

1-EM-1D-13   **Written policy, procedure, and practice encourage and provide for employees to continue their education and training.**

Comment:
None.

SELF-EVALUATION Agency Personnel	STANDARDS COMPLIANCE AUDIT Visiting Committee
Staff Signature(s): _____ _____ ❑ Compliance (list documentation) ❑ Noncompliance (see plan of action) ❑ Not applicable (justification attached) ❑ Plan of action waiver requested (justification attached) Prepare one of the following, as appropriate: 1) List documentation to support compliance; 2) Explain nonapplicability of standard: 3) Explain plan of action waiver request.	Auditor Signature(s): _____ _____ ❑ Compliance ❑ POA acceptable ❑ Noncompliance ❑ POA unacceptable ❑ Not Applicable ❑ Waiver acceptable ❑ Waiver unacceptable List deficiencies if standard is in noncompliance: **NOTE: List all deficiencies if standard is in noncompliance or not applicable. State exactly why standard is in noncompliance. Make complete comments in space above and attach any other information, if necessary. BE VERY SPECIFIC!**

Section E
Case Records

Principle: A written body of policy and procedure establishes the program's management of case records, including security, right of access, and release of information.

Case Records

1-EM-1E-01   **Written policy, procedure, and practice govern case record management, including, at a minimum, the following areas: the establishment, use, and content of case records; right to privacy; secure placement and preservation of records; and schedule for retiring or destroying inactive records. The policies and procedures are reviewed annually.**

Comment:
An orderly and timely system for recording, maintaining, and using data about offenders increases the efficiency and effectiveness of program and service delivery and the transfer of information to the courts and release authorities. The policy should cover the offenders' access to their files.

SELF-EVALUATION Agency Personnel	STANDARDS COMPLIANCE AUDIT Visiting Committee
Staff Signature(s): _____ _____	Auditor Signature(s): _____ _____

Self-Evaluation:
- ❏ Compliance (list documentation)
- ❏ Noncompliance (see plan of action)
- ❏ Not applicable (justification attached)
- ❏ Plan of action waiver requested (justification attached)

Prepare one of the following, as appropriate:

1) List documentation to support compliance;
2) Explain nonapplicability of standard:
3) Explain plan of action waiver request.

Standards Compliance Audit:
- ❏ Compliance
- ❏ Noncompliance
- ❏ Not Applicable
- ❏ POA acceptable
- ❏ POA unacceptable
- ❏ Waiver acceptable
- ❏ Waiver unacceptable

List deficiencies if standard is in noncompliance:

NOTE: List all deficiencies if standard is in noncompliance or not applicable. State exactly why standard is in noncompliance. Make complete comments in space above and attach any other information, if necessary. BE VERY SPECIFIC!

1-EM-1E-02 Written policy, procedure, and practice provide that a record is maintained for each offender and includes, at a minimum, the following information:

- initial intake information form
- case information from referral source, if available
- case history/social history
- medical record, when available
- mental health records/reports, when available
- individual plan or program
- signed release of information forms
- emergency information
- evaluation and progress reports
- current employment data
- program rules and disciplinary policy, signed by offender
- documentation of all contact with offender in person or by telephone and all collateral contacts
- schedule and verification of approved activities
- documented legal authority to accept offender
- grievance and disciplinary record
- referrals to other agencies
- final discharge or transfer report

Comment:
The record is a composite report including background information, ongoing progress reports, and current information. Any staff member should be able to obtain clear and concise knowledge about offenders and their progress through the program records.

SELF-EVALUATION Agency Personnel	STANDARDS COMPLIANCE AUDIT Visiting Committee
Staff Signature(s): _____ _____ ❑ Compliance (list documentation) ❑ Noncompliance (see plan of action) ❑ Not applicable (justification attached) ❑ Plan of action waiver requested (justification attached) Prepare one of the following, as appropriate: 1) List documentation to support compliance; 2) Explain nonapplicability of standard: 3) Explain plan of action waiver request.	Auditor Signature(s): _____ _____ ❑ Compliance ❑ POA acceptable ❑ Noncompliance ❑ POA unacceptable ❑ Not Applicable ❑ Waiver acceptable ❑ Waiver unacceptable List deficiencies if standard is in noncompliance: NOTE: List all deficiencies if standard is in noncompliance or not applicable. State exactly why standard is in noncompliance. Make complete comments in space above and attach any other information, if necessary. BE VERY SPECIFIC!

1-EM-1E-03   **Written policy, procedure, and practice provide for the review of case records at least monthly.**

Comment:
All records must be reviewed on a regular basis by staff to ensure that appropriate and accurate material is being entered. Policy must designate the persons who may have access to these records.

SELF-EVALUATION Agency Personnel	STANDARDS COMPLIANCE AUDIT Visiting Committee
Staff Signature(s):	Auditor Signature(s):
_____ _____	_____ _____
❑ Compliance (list documentation) ❑ Noncompliance (see plan of action) ❑ Not applicable (justification attached) ❑ Plan of action waiver requested (justification attached) Prepare one of the following, as appropriate: 1) List documentation to support compliance; 2) Explain nonapplicability of standard: 3) Explain plan of action waiver request.	❑ Compliance　❑ POA acceptable ❑ Noncompliance　❑ POA unacceptable ❑ Not Applicable　❑ Waiver acceptable 　　　　　　　　❑ Waiver unacceptable List deficiencies if standard is in noncompliance: **NOTE: List all deficiencies if standard is in noncompliance or not applicable. State exactly why standard is in noncompliance. Make complete comments in space above and attach any other information, if necessary. BE VERY SPECIFIC!**

1-EM-1E-04   **Written policy, procedure, and practice require that all entries in the case record are signed and dated. In the case of electronic data, the entry is identified by the author and date.**

Comment:
None.

SELF-EVALUATION Agency Personnel	STANDARDS COMPLIANCE AUDIT Visiting Committee
Staff Signature(s): _____ _____ ❑ Compliance (list documentation) ❑ Noncompliance (see plan of action) ❑ Not applicable (justification attached) ❑ Plan of action waiver requested (justification attached) Prepare one of the following, as appropriate: 1) List documentation to support compliance; 2) Explain nonapplicability of standard: 3) Explain plan of action waiver request.	Auditor Signature(s): _____ _____ ❑ Compliance ❑ POA acceptable ❑ Noncompliance ❑ POA unacceptable ❑ Not Applicable ❑ Waiver acceptable ❑ Waiver unacceptable List deficiencies if standard is in noncompliance: NOTE: List all deficiencies if standard is in noncompliance or not applicable. State exactly why standard is in noncompliance. Make complete comments in space above and attach any other information, if necessary. BE VERY SPECIFIC!

1-EM-1E-05   **Written policy, procedure, and practice provide that appropriate safeguards exist to minimize the possibility of theft, loss, or destruction of records.**

Comment:
All records should be maintained in a secure location, preferably in an office area that has 24-hour staff coverage. Theft, loss, or destruction of records represents a potentially serious setback to the program and often to the offender.

SELF-EVALUATION Agency Personnel	STANDARDS COMPLIANCE AUDIT Visiting Committee
Staff Signature(s): _____ _____ ❏ Compliance (list documentation) ❏ Noncompliance (see plan of action) ❏ Not applicable (justification attached) ❏ Plan of action waiver requested (justification attached) Prepare one of the following, as appropriate: 1) List documentation to support compliance; 2) Explain nonapplicability of standard: 3) Explain plan of action waiver request.	Auditor Signature(s): _____ _____ ❏ Compliance ❏ POA acceptable ❏ Noncompliance ❏ POA unacceptable ❏ Not Applicable ❏ Waiver acceptable ❏ Waiver unacceptable List deficiencies if standard is in noncompliance: **NOTE: List all deficiencies if standard is in noncompliance or not applicable. State exactly why standard is in noncompliance. Make complete comments in space above and attach any other information, if necessary. BE VERY SPECIFIC!**

1-EM-1E-06   **Written policy, procedure, and practice require the backup at least daily of electronic data.**

Comment:
None.

SELF-EVALUATION Agency Personnel	STANDARDS COMPLIANCE AUDIT Visiting Committee
Staff Signature(s): _____ _____ ❑ Compliance (list documentation) ❑ Noncompliance (see plan of action) ❑ Not applicable (justification attached) ❑ Plan of action waiver requested (justification attached) Prepare one of the following, as appropriate: 1) List documentation to support compliance; 2) Explain nonapplicability of standard: 3) Explain plan of action waiver request.	Auditor Signature(s): _____ _____ ❑ Compliance ❑ POA acceptable ❑ Noncompliance ❑ POA unacceptable ❑ Not Applicable ❑ Waiver acceptable ❑ Waiver unacceptable List deficiencies if standard is in noncompliance: **NOTE: List all deficiencies if standard is in noncompliance or not applicable. State exactly why standard is in noncompliance. Make complete comments in space above and attach any other information, if necessary. BE VERY SPECIFIC!**

Confidentiality

1-EM-1E-07   **Written policy, procedure, and practice provide that records are safeguarded from unauthorized and improper disclosure and that when any part of the information system is computerized, security ensures confidentiality.**

Comment:
An offender's constitutional right to privacy can be violated if records are improperly disseminated. The program should establish procedures to limit access to records to persons and public agencies that have both a "need to know" and a "right to know" and can demonstrate that access to such information is necessary for criminal justice purposes. Written guidelines should regulate offenders' access to records.

SELF-EVALUATION Agency Personnel	STANDARDS COMPLIANCE AUDIT Visiting Committee
Staff Signature(s): _____ _____	Auditor Signature(s): _____ _____
❏ Compliance (list documentation) ❏ Noncompliance (see plan of action) ❏ Not applicable (justification attached) ❏ Plan of action waiver requested (justification attached) Prepare one of the following, as appropriate: 1) List documentation to support compliance; 2) Explain nonapplicability of standard: 3) Explain plan of action waiver request.	❏ Compliance ❏ POA acceptable ❏ Noncompliance ❏ POA unacceptable ❏ Not Applicable ❏ Waiver acceptable ❏ Waiver unacceptable List deficiencies if standard is in noncompliance: **NOTE: List all deficiencies if standard is in noncompliance or not applicable. State exactly why standard is in noncompliance. Make complete comments in space above and attach any other information, if necessary. BE VERY SPECIFIC!**

Access to Records

1-EM-1E-08   **Written policy, procedure, and practice govern offenders' access to information in their case records.**

Comment:
Offenders should have access to their case records and files consistent with applicable statutes regarding procedures and conditions for reviewing these materials. Exceptions should be based on possible harm to the offender or others.

SELF-EVALUATION Agency Personnel	STANDARDS COMPLIANCE AUDIT Visiting Committee
Staff Signature(s): _____ _____ ❑ Compliance (list documentation) ❑ Noncompliance (see plan of action) ❑ Not applicable (justification attached) ❑ Plan of action waiver requested (justification attached) Prepare one of the following, as appropriate: 1) List documentation to support compliance; 2) Explain nonapplicability of standard: 3) Explain plan of action waiver request.	Auditor Signature(s): _____ _____ ❑ Compliance ❑ POA acceptable ❑ Noncompliance ❑ POA unacceptable ❑ Not Applicable ❑ Waiver acceptable ❑ Waiver unacceptable List deficiencies if standard is in noncompliance: **NOTE: List all deficiencies if standard is in noncompliance or not applicable. State exactly why standard is in noncompliance. Make complete comments in space above and attach any other information, if necessary. BE VERY SPECIFIC!**

Release of Information

1-EM-1E-09   **Written policy, procedure, and practice provide that the program uses a "release of information consent form" that complies with applicable federal and state regulations. A copy of the form is maintained in the offender's case record.**

Comment:
None.

SELF-EVALUATION Agency Personnel	STANDARDS COMPLIANCE AUDIT Visiting Committee
Staff Signature(s):	Auditor Signature(s):
_____	_____
_____	_____
❑ Compliance (list documentation) ❑ Noncompliance (see plan of action) ❑ Not applicable (justification attached) ❑ Plan of action waiver requested (justification attached)	❑ Compliance ❑ POA acceptable ❑ Noncompliance ❑ POA unacceptable ❑ Not Applicable ❑ Waiver acceptable ❑ Waiver unacceptable
Prepare one of the following, as appropriate: 1) List documentation to support compliance; 2) Explain nonapplicability of standard: 3) Explain plan of action waiver request.	List deficiencies if standard is in noncompliance: **NOTE: List all deficiencies if standard is in noncompliance or not applicable. State exactly why standard is in noncompliance. Make complete comments in space above and attach any other information, if necessary. BE VERY SPECIFIC!**

Section F
Information Systems and Research

Principle: A written body of policy and procedure establishes the program's information systems and research programs.

Information Systems

1-EM-1F-01   **Written policy, procedure, and practice govern access to and use of an organized system of information collection, storage, retrieval, reporting, and review.**

Comment:
The system should be only as complex and sophisticated as the program's size, complexity, and resources warrant.

SELF-EVALUATION Agency Personnel	STANDARDS COMPLIANCE AUDIT Visiting Committee
Staff Signature(s): _____ _____	Auditor Signature(s): _____ _____
❏ Compliance (list documentation) ❏ Noncompliance (see plan of action) ❏ Not applicable (justification attached) ❏ Plan of action waiver requested (justification attached) Prepare one of the following, as appropriate: 1) List documentation to support compliance; 2) Explain nonapplicability of standard: 3) Explain plan of action waiver request.	❏ Compliance ❏ POA acceptable ❏ Noncompliance ❏ POA unacceptable ❏ Not Applicable ❏ Waiver acceptable ❏ Waiver unacceptable List deficiencies if standard is in noncompliance: **NOTE: List all deficiencies if standard is in noncompliance or not applicable. State exactly why standard is in noncompliance. Make complete comments in space above and attach any other information, if necessary. BE VERY SPECIFIC!**

1-EM-1F-02   **Written policy, procedure, and practice provide that the program cooperates with other criminal justice agencies in the gathering, exchanging, and standardizing of information.**

Comment:
Systemwide cooperation is critical to effective management and timely decision making and helps prevent or reduce duplication of effort. Facilities should share information while respecting the confidentiality and privacy of offender records.

SELF-EVALUATION Agency Personnel	STANDARDS COMPLIANCE AUDIT Visiting Committee
Staff Signature(s): _____ _____	Auditor Signature(s): _____ _____

Self-Evaluation column:

❑ Compliance (list documentation)
❑ Noncompliance (see plan of action)
❑ Not applicable (justification attached)
❑ Plan of action waiver requested (justification attached)

Prepare one of the following, as appropriate:

1) List documentation to support compliance;
2) Explain nonapplicability of standard:
3) Explain plan of action waiver request.

Standards Compliance Audit column:

❑ Compliance   ❑ POA acceptable
❑ Noncompliance   ❑ POA unacceptable
❑ Not Applicable   ❑ Waiver acceptable
                      ❑ Waiver unacceptable

List deficiencies if standard is in noncompliance:

NOTE: List all deficiencies if standard is in noncompliance or not applicable. State exactly why standard is in noncompliance. Make complete comments in space above and attach any other information, if necessary. BE VERY SPECIFIC!

1-EM-1F-03   **Written policy, procedure, and practice provide for an annual evaluation of information systems and research operations and progress toward goals and objectives.**

Comment:
None.

SELF-EVALUATION Agency Personnel	STANDARDS COMPLIANCE AUDIT Visiting Committee
Staff Signature(s): _____ _____ ❏ Compliance (list documentation) ❏ Noncompliance (see plan of action) ❏ Not applicable (justification attached) ❏ Plan of action waiver requested (justification attached) Prepare one of the following, as appropriate: 1) List documentation to support compliance; 2) Explain nonapplicability of standard: 3) Explain plan of action waiver request.	Auditor Signature(s): _____ _____ ❏ Compliance ❏ POA acceptable ❏ Noncompliance ❏ POA unacceptable ❏ Not Applicable ❏ Waiver acceptable ❏ Waiver unacceptable List deficiencies if standard is in noncompliance: **NOTE: List all deficiencies if standard is in noncompliance or not applicable. State exactly why standard is in noncompliance. Make complete comments in space above and attach any other information, if necessary. BE VERY SPECIFIC!**

1-EM-1F-04   **Written policy, procedure, and practice govern the security of the information and data collection system, including verification, access to data, and protection of the privacy of offenders.**

Comment:
Procedures should be specified not only for verifying data before it is entered into the system, but also for determining what data are required. Written policy should specify those persons who have access to the information system.

SELF-EVALUATION Agency Personnel	STANDARDS COMPLIANCE AUDIT Visiting Committee
Staff Signature(s): _____ _____ ❏ Compliance (list documentation) ❏ Noncompliance (see plan of action) ❏ Not applicable (justification attached) ❏ Plan of action waiver requested (justification attached) Prepare one of the following, as appropriate: 1) List documentation to support compliance; 2) Explain nonapplicability of standard: 3) Explain plan of action waiver request.	Auditor Signature(s): _____ _____ ❏ Compliance ❏ POA acceptable ❏ Noncompliance ❏ POA unacceptable ❏ Not Applicable ❏ Waiver acceptable ❏ Waiver unacceptable List deficiencies if standard is in noncompliance: **NOTE: List all deficiencies if standard is in noncompliance or not applicable. State exactly why standard is in noncompliance. Make complete comments in space above and attach any other information, if necessary. BE VERY SPECIFIC!**

Research Activities

1-EM-1F-05 **Written policy, procedure, and practice provide that the program or parent agency supports, engages, and uses research activities relevant to its programs, services, and operations.**

Comment:
Research can assist in planning and establishing goals and objectives. Controlled studies, evaluations, and policy research can contribute to more efficient and effective program operations, programs, and services and help increase public safety.

SELF-EVALUATION Agency Personnel	STANDARDS COMPLIANCE AUDIT Visiting Committee
Staff Signature(s):	Auditor Signature(s):
❑ Compliance (list documentation) ❑ Noncompliance (see plan of action) ❑ Not applicable (justification attached) ❑ Plan of action waiver requested (justification attached) Prepare one of the following, as appropriate: 1) List documentation to support compliance; 2) Explain nonapplicability of standard: 3) Explain plan of action waiver request.	❑ Compliance ❑ POA acceptable ❑ Noncompliance ❑ POA unacceptable ❑ Not Applicable ❑ Waiver acceptable ❑ Waiver unacceptable List deficiencies if standard is in noncompliance: NOTE: List all deficiencies if standard is in noncompliance or not applicable. State exactly why standard is in noncompliance. Make complete comments in space above and attach any other information, if necessary. BE VERY SPECIFIC!

1-EM-1F-06 **Written policy, procedure, and practice provide that the program administrator reviews and approves all research projects prior to implementation.**

Comment:
Research should not be permitted to proceed until the research design and requirements of the program staff are understood and fully agreed upon.

SELF-EVALUATION Agency Personnel	STANDARDS COMPLIANCE AUDIT Visiting Committee
Staff Signature(s): _____ _____ ❑ Compliance (list documentation) ❑ Noncompliance (see plan of action) ❑ Not applicable (justification attached) ❑ Plan of action waiver requested (justification attached) Prepare one of the following, as appropriate: 1) List documentation to support compliance; 2) Explain nonapplicability of standard: 3) Explain plan of action waiver request.	Auditor Signature(s): _____ _____ ❑ Compliance ❑ POA acceptable ❑ Noncompliance ❑ POA unacceptable ❑ Not Applicable ❑ Waiver acceptable ❑ Waiver unacceptable List deficiencies if standard is in noncompliance: **NOTE: List all deficiencies if standard is in noncompliance or not applicable. State exactly why standard is in noncompliance. Make complete comments in space above and attach any other information, if necessary. BE VERY SPECIFIC!**

Conduct of Research

1-EM-1F-07   **Written policy, procedure, and practice governing the conduct of research in the program comply with state and federal guidelines for the use and dissemination of research findings and comply with accepted professional and scientific ethics and issues of legal consent and release of information.**

Comment:
Researchers working in the program should be informed of all policies relating to their research, especially those regarding confidentiality of information.

SELF-EVALUATION Agency Personnel	STANDARDS COMPLIANCE AUDIT Visiting Committee
Staff Signature(s): _____ _____ ❑ Compliance (list documentation) ❑ Noncompliance (see plan of action) ❑ Not applicable (justification attached) ❑ Plan of action waiver requested (justification attached) Prepare one of the following, as appropriate: 1) List documentation to support compliance; 2) Explain nonapplicability of standard: 3) Explain plan of action waiver request.	Auditor Signature(s): _____ _____ ❑ Compliance ❑ POA acceptable ❑ Noncompliance ❑ POA unacceptable ❑ Not Applicable ❑ Waiver acceptable ❑ Waiver unacceptable List deficiencies if standard is in noncompliance: **NOTE: List all deficiencies if standard is in noncompliance or not applicable. State exactly why standard is in noncompliance. Make complete comments in space above and attach any other information, if necessary. BE VERY SPECIFIC!**

1-EM-1F-08   **Written policy, procedure, and practice provide that all research results are made available to the program administrator for review and comment prior to publication or dissemination.**

Comment:
None.

SELF-EVALUATION Agency Personnel	STANDARDS COMPLIANCE AUDIT Visiting Committee
Staff Signature(s): _____ _____	Auditor Signature(s): _____ _____

Self-Evaluation:

❑ Compliance (list documentation)
❑ Noncompliance (see plan of action)
❑ Not applicable (justification attached)
❑ Plan of action waiver requested (justification attached)

Prepare one of the following, as appropriate:

1) List documentation to support compliance;
2) Explain nonapplicability of standard:
3) Explain plan of action waiver request.

Standards Compliance Audit:

❑ Compliance   ❑ POA acceptable
❑ Noncompliance   ❑ POA unacceptable
❑ Not Applicable   ❑ Waiver acceptable
                    ❑ Waiver unacceptable

List deficiencies if standard is in noncompliance:

NOTE: List all deficiencies if standard is in noncompliance or not applicable. State exactly why standard is in noncompliance. Make complete comments in space above and attach any other information, if necessary. BE VERY SPECIFIC!

Offender Participation in Research

1-EM-1F-09   **Written policy, procedure, and practice govern the voluntary participation of offenders in nonmedical, nonpharmaceutical, and noncosmetic research programs.**

Comment:
None.

SELF-EVALUATION Agency Personnel	STANDARDS COMPLIANCE AUDIT Visiting Committee
Staff Signature(s): _____ _____ ❑ Compliance (list documentation) ❑ Noncompliance (see plan of action) ❑ Not applicable (justification attached) ❑ Plan of action waiver requested (justification attached) Prepare one of the following, as appropriate: 1) List documentation to support compliance; 2) Explain nonapplicability of standard: 3) Explain plan of action waiver request.	Auditor Signature(s): _____ _____ ❑ Compliance ❑ POA acceptable ❑ Noncompliance ❑ POA unacceptable ❑ Not Applicable ❑ Waiver acceptable 　　　　　　　　　❑ Waiver unacceptable List deficiencies if standard is in noncompliance: **NOTE: List all deficiencies if standard is in noncompliance or not applicable. State exactly why standard is in noncompliance. Make complete comments in space above and attach any other information, if necessary. BE VERY SPECIFIC!**

1-EM-1F-10
Mandatory

Written policy prohibits the use of offenders for medical, pharmaceutical, or cosmetic experiments. This policy does not preclude individual treatment of an offender based on the offender's need for a specific medical procedure that is not generally available.

Comment:
A person confined in a program is incapable of volunteering as a human subject without hope of reward and cannot do so based on fully informed consent. Therefore, offenders should not participate in experimental projects involving medical, pharmaceutical, or cosmetic research, including aversive conditioning, psychosurgery, electrical stimulation of the brain, or the application of cosmetic substances to the body that are being tested for possible ill effects prior to sale to the general public. This does not preclude individual treatment of an offender by his/her physician with a new medical procedure, subsequent to a full explanation of the positive and negative features of the treatment. The agreement is between the physician and the offender and is not part of a general program of medical experimentation involving payment to offenders for submission to treatment.

SELF-EVALUATION Agency Personnel	STANDARDS COMPLIANCE AUDIT Visiting Committee
Staff Signature(s):	Auditor Signature(s):
❏ Compliance (list documentation) ❏ Noncompliance (see plan of action) ❏ Not applicable (justification attached) ❏ Plan of action waiver requested (justification attached)	❏ Compliance ❏ POA acceptable ❏ Noncompliance ❏ POA unacceptable ❏ Not Applicable ❏ Waiver acceptable ❏ Waiver unacceptable
Prepare one of the following, as appropriate: 1) List documentation to support compliance; 2) Explain nonapplicability of standard: 3) Explain plan of action waiver request.	List deficiencies if standard is in noncompliance: **NOTE: List all deficiencies if standard is in noncompliance or not applicable. State exactly why standard is in noncompliance. Make complete comments in space above and attach any other information, if necessary. BE VERY SPECIFIC!**

Part Two
Physical Plant

Section A
Building and Safety Codes

Principle: Compliance with appropriate codes ensures the quality and safety of the program.

Building Codes

1-EM-2A-01   **Written policy, procedure, and practice provide that the program facility conforms to all applicable building codes.**

Comment:
Often a state or local jurisdiction will license a program, thereby indicating the program facility complies with all building codes. In those cases when a license is not issued, letters or certificates of compliance are acceptable. In the event the program is not subject to local (city and/or county) building codes, state codes will be applied.

SELF-EVALUATION **Agency Personnel**	**STANDARDS COMPLIANCE AUDIT** **Visiting Committee**
Staff Signature(s): _____ _____	Auditor Signature(s): _____ _____
❏ Compliance (list documentation) ❏ Noncompliance (see plan of action) ❏ Not applicable (justification attached) ❏ Plan of action waiver requested (justification attached) Prepare one of the following, as appropriate: 1) List documentation to support compliance; 2) Explain nonapplicability of standard; 3) Explain plan of action waiver request.	❏ Compliance ❏ POA acceptable ❏ Noncompliance ❏ POA unacceptable ❏ Not Applicable ❏ Waiver acceptable ❏ Waiver unacceptable List deficiencies if standard is in noncompliance: **NOTE: List all deficiencies if standard is in noncompliance or not applicable. State exactly why standard is in noncompliance. Make complete comments in space above and attach any other information, if necessary. BE VERY SPECIFIC!**

1-EM-2A-02   **Written policy, procedure, and practice provide that the program facility conforms to all applicable zoning ordinances.**

Comment:
Most agencies must comply with zoning ordinances before receiving permission to move into a program facility. However, some agencies receive provisional approval, based upon hearings, appeals, and changes in ordinances. If this is the case, the program must show it is making efforts to comply.

SELF-EVALUATION Agency Personnel	STANDARDS COMPLIANCE AUDIT Visiting Committee
Staff Signature(s): _____ _____	Auditor Signature(s): _____ _____
❑ Compliance (list documentation) ❑ Noncompliance (see plan of action) ❑ Not applicable (justification attached) ❑ Plan of action waiver requested (justification attached) Prepare one of the following, as appropriate: 1) List documentation to support compliance; 2) Explain nonapplicability of standard: 3) Explain plan of action waiver request.	❑ Compliance ❑ POA acceptable ❑ Noncompliance ❑ POA unacceptable ❑ Not Applicable ❑ Waiver acceptable ❑ Waiver unacceptable List deficiencies if standard is in noncompliance: **NOTE: List all deficiencies if standard is in noncompliance or not applicable. State exactly why standard is in noncompliance. Make complete comments in space above and attach any other information, if necessary. BE VERY SPECIFIC!**

Fire Codes

1-EM-2A-03
Mandatory

Written policy, procedure, and practice provide that the program facility complies with the regulations of the fire authority having jurisdiction.

Comment:
Local and state fire codes must be adhered to in order to ensure the safety of offenders and the staff. Reports of periodic inspections and action taken should be maintained.

SELF-EVALUATION Agency Personnel	STANDARDS COMPLIANCE AUDIT Visiting Committee
Staff Signature(s): _____ _____	Auditor Signature(s): _____ _____

Self-Evaluation:

❏ Compliance (list documentation)
❏ Noncompliance (see plan of action)
❏ Not applicable (justification attached)
❏ Plan of action waiver requested (justification attached)

Prepare one of the following, as appropriate:

1) List documentation to support compliance;
2) Explain nonapplicability of standard:
3) Explain plan of action waiver request.

Standards Compliance Audit:

❏ Compliance   ❏ POA acceptable
❏ Noncompliance   ❏ POA unacceptable
❏ Not Applicable   ❏ Waiver acceptable
                   ❏ Waiver unacceptable

List deficiencies if standard is in noncompliance:

NOTE: List all deficiencies if standard is in noncompliance or not applicable. State exactly why standard is in noncompliance. Make complete comments in space above and attach any other information, if necessary. BE VERY SPECIFIC!

Part Three
Program Operations

Section A
Supervision

Principle: The program uses a combination of supervision, accountability, and policies and procedures to promote safe and orderly operations.

Operations Manual

1-EM-3A-01   **There is a manual containing all procedures for the supervision of offenders with detailed instructions for their implementation. The manual is available to all staff and is reviewed at least annually and updated, if necessary.**

Comment:
The manual should contain information on emergency procedures and responses to indications that the offender is out of range, the offender's phone is disabled, power and telephone outages, and other situations that might indicate violations of the program's requirements.

SELF-EVALUATION Agency Personnel	STANDARDS COMPLIANCE AUDIT Visiting Committee
Staff Signature(s): _____ _____	Auditor Signature(s): _____ _____
❑ Compliance (list documentation) ❑ Noncompliance (see plan of action) ❑ Not applicable (justification attached) ❑ Plan of action waiver requested (justification attached) Prepare one of the following, as appropriate: 1) List documentation to support compliance; 2) Explain nonapplicability of standard: 3) Explain plan of action waiver request.	❑ Compliance ❑ POA acceptable ❑ Noncompliance ❑ POA unacceptable ❑ Not Applicable ❑ Waiver acceptable ❑ Waiver unacceptable List deficiencies if standard is in noncompliance: **NOTE: List all deficiencies if standard is in noncompliance or not applicable. State exactly why standard is in noncompliance. Make complete comments in space above and attach any other information, if necessary. BE VERY SPECIFIC!**

Staff Availability

1-EM-3A-02   Written policy, procedure, and practice provide that the staffing pattern is developed to ensure appropriate staff to maximize accountability.

Comment:
None.

SELF-EVALUATION Agency Personnel	STANDARDS COMPLIANCE AUDIT Visiting Committee
Staff Signature(s):	Auditor Signature(s):
_____ _____	_____ _____
❏ Compliance (list documentation) ❏ Noncompliance (see plan of action) ❏ Not applicable (justification attached) ❏ Plan of action waiver requested (justification attached) Prepare one of the following, as appropriate: 1) List documentation to support compliance; 2) Explain nonapplicability of standard: 3) Explain plan of action waiver request.	❏ Compliance ❏ POA acceptable ❏ Noncompliance ❏ POA unacceptable ❏ Not Applicable ❏ Waiver acceptable ❏ Waiver unacceptable List deficiencies if standard is in noncompliance: NOTE: List all deficiencies if standard is in noncompliance or not applicable. State exactly why standard is in noncompliance. Make complete comments in space above and attach any other information, if necessary. BE VERY SPECIFIC!

1-EM-3A-03   **Written policy, procedure, and practice require that staff maintain a permanent log and prepare shift reports that record routine information, emergency situations, and unusual incidents.**

Comment:
Adequate supervision of offenders requires an accurate, written reporting system.

SELF-EVALUATION Agency Personnel	STANDARDS COMPLIANCE AUDIT Visiting Committee
Staff Signature(s):	Auditor Signature(s):

Self-evaluation:

❏ Compliance (list documentation)
❏ Noncompliance (see plan of action)
❏ Not applicable (justification attached)
❏ Plan of action waiver requested (justification attached)

Prepare one of the following, as appropriate:

1) List documentation to support compliance;
2) Explain nonapplicability of standard:
3) Explain plan of action waiver request.

Standards compliance audit:

❏ Compliance   ❏ POA acceptable
❏ Noncompliance   ❏ POA unacceptable
❏ Not Applicable   ❏ Waiver acceptable
                   ❏ Waiver unacceptable

List deficiencies if standard is in noncompliance:

NOTE: List all deficiencies if standard is in noncompliance or not applicable. State exactly why standard is in noncompliance. Make complete comments in space above and attach any other information, if necessary. BE VERY SPECIFIC!

Offender Control

1-EM-3A-04   **Written policy, procedure, and practice provide that the program has a system of accounting for an offender at all times, including verification of activities, reporting of tardiness and/or absence from required services or activities, as well as other program violations.**

Comment:
An accountability system for offenders must be established.

SELF-EVALUATION Agency Personnel	STANDARDS COMPLIANCE AUDIT Visiting Committee
Staff Signature(s): _____ _____ ❑ Compliance (list documentation) ❑ Noncompliance (see plan of action) ❑ Not applicable (justification attached) ❑ Plan of action waiver requested (justification attached) Prepare one of the following, as appropriate: 1) List documentation to support compliance; 2) Explain nonapplicability of standard: 3) Explain plan of action waiver request.	Auditor Signature(s): _____ _____ ❑ Compliance ❑ POA acceptable ❑ Noncompliance ❑ POA unacceptable ❑ Not Applicable ❑ Waiver acceptable ❑ Waiver unacceptable List deficiencies if standard is in noncompliance: **NOTE: List all deficiencies if standard is in noncompliance or not applicable. State exactly why standard is in noncompliance. Make complete comments in space above and attach any other information, if necessary. BE VERY SPECIFIC!**

1-EM-3A-05   **Written policy, procedure, and practice provide that no offender or group of offenders is in a position of control or authority over other offenders.**

Comment:
Under no circumstances should offenders be used or allowed to control others. There are instances when a supervised system of advanced responsibilities for offenders may be used.

SELF-EVALUATION Agency Personnel	STANDARDS COMPLIANCE AUDIT Visiting Committee

Staff Signature(s):

_____

_____

❑ Compliance (list documentation)
❑ Noncompliance (see plan of action)
❑ Not applicable (justification attached)
❑ Plan of action waiver requested (justification attached)

Prepare one of the following, as appropriate:

1) List documentation to support compliance;
2) Explain nonapplicability of standard:
3) Explain plan of action waiver request.

Auditor Signature(s):

_____

_____

❑ Compliance   ❑ POA acceptable
❑ Noncompliance   ❑ POA unacceptable
❑ Not Applicable   ❑ Waiver acceptable
                              ❑ Waiver unacceptable

List deficiencies if standard is in noncompliance:

NOTE: List all deficiencies if standard is in noncompliance or not applicable. State exactly why standard is in noncompliance. Make complete comments in space above and attach any other information, if necessary. BE VERY SPECIFIC!

1-EM-3A-06　　**Written policy, procedure, and practice provide that all activity schedule changes are made only by authorized personnel, and those changes reflect the name of the person with authorization to make the changes.**

Comment:
None.

SELF-EVALUATION Agency Personnel	STANDARDS COMPLIANCE AUDIT Visiting Committee
Staff Signature(s):	Auditor Signature(s):
_____	_____
❑ Compliance (list documentation) ❑ Noncompliance (see plan of action) ❑ Not applicable (justification attached) ❑ Plan of action waiver requested (justification attached)	❑ Compliance　　❑ POA acceptable ❑ Noncompliance　❑ POA unacceptable ❑ Not Applicable　❑ Waiver acceptable 　　　　　　　　❑ Waiver unacceptable
Prepare one of the following, as appropriate: 1) List documentation to support compliance; 2) Explain nonapplicability of standard: 3) Explain plan of action waiver request.	List deficiencies if standard is in noncompliance:
	NOTE: List all deficiencies if standard is in noncompliance or not applicable. State exactly why standard is in noncompliance. Make complete comments in space above and attach any other information, if necessary. BE VERY SPECIFIC!

Section B
Safety and Emergency Procedures

Principle: The program has the necessary equipment and procedures in place in the event of a major emergency.

Emergency Equipment

1-EM-3B-01 **The program base station has adequate power and communication backup systems to provide continuous, uninterrupted operations.**

Comment:
None.

SELF-EVALUATION Agency Personnel	STANDARDS COMPLIANCE AUDIT Visiting Committee
Staff Signature(s): _____ _____	Auditor Signature(s): _____ _____
❏ Compliance (list documentation) ❏ Noncompliance (see plan of action) ❏ Not applicable (justification attached) ❏ Plan of action waiver requested (justification attached) Prepare one of the following, as appropriate: 1) List documentation to support compliance; 2) Explain nonapplicability of standard: 3) Explain plan of action waiver request.	❏ Compliance ❏ POA acceptable ❏ Noncompliance ❏ POA unacceptable ❏ Not Applicable ❏ Waiver acceptable ❏ Waiver unacceptable List deficiencies if standard is in noncompliance: **NOTE: List all deficiencies if standard is in noncompliance or not applicable. State exactly why standard is in noncompliance. Make complete comments in space above and attach any other information, if necessary. BE VERY SPECIFIC!**

Emergency Plans

1-EM-3B-02   **Written policy, procedure, and practice provide that all personnel are trained in the implementation of emergency plans.**

Comment:
Since staff must be able to properly execute the plans, a review of the emergency plans should be an essential element of personnel orientation and in-service training.

SELF-EVALUATION **Agency Personnel**	**STANDARDS COMPLIANCE AUDIT** **Visiting Committee**
Staff Signature(s):	Auditor Signature(s):
_____ _____	_____ _____
❑ Compliance (list documentation) ❑ Noncompliance (see plan of action) ❑ Not applicable (justification attached) ❑ Plan of action waiver requested (justification attached) Prepare one of the following, as appropriate: 1) List documentation to support compliance; 2) Explain nonapplicability of standard: 3) Explain plan of action waiver request.	❑ Compliance ❑ POA acceptable ❑ Noncompliance ❑ POA unacceptable ❑ Not Applicable ❑ Waiver acceptable ❑ Waiver unacceptable List deficiencies if standard is in noncompliance: NOTE: List all deficiencies if standard is in noncompliance or not applicable. State exactly why standard is in noncompliance. Make complete comments in space above and attach any other information, if necessary. **BE VERY SPECIFIC!**

1-EM-3B-03   **Written policy, procedure, and practice describe the retrieval of offender information during an emergency.**

Comment:
None.

SELF-EVALUATION Agency Personnel	STANDARDS COMPLIANCE AUDIT Visiting Committee
Staff Signature(s): _____ _____ ❏ Compliance (list documentation) ❏ Noncompliance (see plan of action) ❏ Not applicable (justification attached) ❏ Plan of action waiver requested (justification attached) Prepare one of the following, as appropriate: 1) List documentation to support compliance; 2) Explain nonapplicability of standard: 3) Explain plan of action waiver request.	Auditor Signature(s): _____ _____ ❏ Compliance ❏ POA acceptable ❏ Noncompliance ❏ POA unacceptable ❏ Not Applicable ❏ Waiver acceptable ❏ Waiver unacceptable List deficiencies if standard is in noncompliance: **NOTE: List all deficiencies if standard is in noncompliance or not applicable. State exactly why standard is in noncompliance. Make complete comments in space above and attach any other information, if necessary. BE VERY SPECIFIC!**

1-EM-3B-04   **Written policy, procedure, and practice provide that any interruption in service is documented and reported to the authority having jurisdiction.**

Comment:
None.

SELF-EVALUATION Agency Personnel	STANDARDS COMPLIANCE AUDIT Visiting Committee
Staff Signature(s): _____ _____ ❑ Compliance (list documentation) ❑ Noncompliance (see plan of action) ❑ Not applicable (justification attached) ❑ Plan of action waiver requested (justification attached) Prepare one of the following, as appropriate: 1) List documentation to support compliance; 2) Explain nonapplicability of standard: 3) Explain plan of action waiver request.	Auditor Signature(s): _____ _____ ❑ Compliance ❑ POA acceptable ❑ Noncompliance ❑ POA unacceptable ❑ Not Applicable ❑ Waiver acceptable ❑ Waiver unacceptable List deficiencies if standard is in noncompliance: **NOTE: List all deficiencies if standard is in noncompliance or not applicable. State exactly why standard is in noncompliance. Make complete comments in space above and attach any other information, if necessary. BE VERY SPECIFIC!**

Flammable, Toxic, and Caustic Materials

1-EM-3B-05
Mandatory

Written policy, procedure, and practice govern the control and use of all flammable, toxic, and caustic materials.

Comment:
None.

SELF-EVALUATION Agency Personnel	STANDARDS COMPLIANCE AUDIT Visiting Committee
Staff Signature(s): _____ _____ ❑ Compliance (list documentation) ❑ Noncompliance (see plan of action) ❑ Not applicable (justification attached) ❑ Plan of action waiver requested (justification attached) Prepare one of the following, as appropriate: 1) List documentation to support compliance; 2) Explain nonapplicability of standard: 3) Explain plan of action waiver request.	Auditor Signature(s): _____ _____ ❑ Compliance ❑ POA acceptable ❑ Noncompliance ❑ POA unacceptable ❑ Not Applicable ❑ Waiver acceptable ❑ Waiver unacceptable List deficiencies if standard is in noncompliance: **NOTE: List all deficiencies if standard is in noncompliance or not applicable. State exactly why standard is in noncompliance. Make complete comments in space above and attach any other information, if necessary. BE VERY SPECIFIC!**

Program Equipment

1-EM-3B-06   **Written policy, procedure, and practice provide that access to computer equipment is limited to authorized personnel with security codes.**

Comment:
None.

SELF-EVALUATION Agency Personnel	STANDARDS COMPLIANCE AUDIT Visiting Committee
Staff Signature(s):	Auditor Signature(s):
_____ _____	_____ _____
❑ Compliance (list documentation) ❑ Noncompliance (see plan of action) ❑ Not applicable (justification attached) ❑ Plan of action waiver requested (justification attached) Prepare one of the following, as appropriate: 1) List documentation to support compliance; 2) Explain nonapplicability of standard: 3) Explain plan of action waiver request.	❑ Compliance ❑ POA acceptable ❑ Noncompliance ❑ POA unacceptable ❑ Not Applicable ❑ Waiver acceptable ❑ Waiver unacceptable List deficiencies if standard is in noncompliance: **NOTE: List all deficiencies if standard is in noncompliance or not applicable. State exactly why standard is in noncompliance. Make complete comments in space above and attach any other information, if necessary. BE VERY SPECIFIC!**

1-EM-3B-07   **Written policy, procedure, and practice provide for the perpetual inventory and preventive maintenance of electronic monitoring equipment for field use.**

Comment:
None.

SELF-EVALUATION Agency Personnel	STANDARDS COMPLIANCE AUDIT Visiting Committee
Staff Signature(s): _____ _____ ❑ Compliance (list documentation) ❑ Noncompliance (see plan of action) ❑ Not applicable (justification attached) ❑ Plan of action waiver requested (justification attached) Prepare one of the following, as appropriate: 1) List documentation to support compliance; 2) Explain nonapplicability of standard: 3) Explain plan of action waiver request.	Auditor Signature(s): _____ _____ ❑ Compliance ❑ POA acceptable ❑ Noncompliance ❑ POA unacceptable ❑ Not Applicable ❑ Waiver acceptable ❑ Waiver unacceptable List deficiencies if standard is in noncompliance: **NOTE: List all deficiencies if standard is in noncompliance or not applicable. State exactly why standard is in noncompliance. Make complete comments in space above and attach any other information, if necessary. BE VERY SPECIFIC!**

Program Transportation

1-EM-3B-08 **For those programs providing vehicles, written policy, procedure, and practice require, at a minimum, an annual safety inspection by qualified individuals. Documentation of immediate completion of safety repairs shall be on file.**

Comment:
Written policy should ensure that program vehicles are operated only by licensed drivers and that vehicles and drivers are insured in conformance with state statutes. All vehicles should be maintained in a safe operating condition and should undergo periodic safety inspections where applicable.

SELF-EVALUATION Agency Personnel	STANDARDS COMPLIANCE AUDIT Visiting Committee
Staff Signature(s): _____ _____	Auditor Signature(s): _____ _____
❏ Compliance (list documentation) ❏ Noncompliance (see plan of action) ❏ Not applicable (justification attached) ❏ Plan of action waiver requested (justification attached) Prepare one of the following, as appropriate: 1) List documentation to support compliance; 2) Explain nonapplicability of standard: 3) Explain plan of action waiver request.	❏ Compliance ❏ POA acceptable ❏ Noncompliance ❏ POA unacceptable ❏ Not Applicable ❏ Waiver acceptable ❏ Waiver unacceptable List deficiencies if standard is in noncompliance: **NOTE: List all deficiencies if standard is in noncompliance or not applicable. State exactly why standard is in noncompliance. Make complete comments in space above and attach any other information, if necessary. BE VERY SPECIFIC!**

Section C
Rules and Discipline

Principle: The program's rules of conduct and sanctions and procedures for violations are defined in writing and communicated to all offenders and staff. Disciplinary procedures are carried out promptly and with respect for the offenders.

Rules of Conduct

1-EM-3C-01   **Written policy, procedure, and practice provide for disciplinary regulations governing offender rule violations, sanctions, and penalties that can be imposed for various degrees of violation. These are reviewed at least annually and updated if necessary.**

Comment:
The regulations should specify the range of penalties/sanctions that can be imposed for violations. Penalties should be proportionate to the importance of the rule and severity of the violation.

SELF-EVALUATION Agency Personnel	STANDARDS COMPLIANCE AUDIT Visiting Committee
Staff Signature(s): _____ _____	Auditor Signature(s): _____ _____

Self-Evaluation:

❑ Compliance (list documentation)
❑ Noncompliance (see plan of action)
❑ Not applicable (justification attached)
❑ Plan of action waiver requested (justification attached)

Prepare one of the following, as appropriate:

1) List documentation to support compliance;
2) Explain nonapplicability of standard:
3) Explain plan of action waiver request.

Standards Compliance Audit:

❑ Compliance   ❑ POA acceptable
❑ Noncompliance ❑ POA unacceptable
❑ Not Applicable ❑ Waiver acceptable
                 ❑ Waiver unacceptable

List deficiencies if standard is in noncompliance:

NOTE: List all deficiencies if standard is in noncompliance or not applicable. State exactly why standard is in noncompliance. Make complete comments in space above and attach any other information, if necessary. BE VERY SPECIFIC!

1-EM-3C-02   **Written policy, procedure, and practice provide that all program rules and regulations pertaining to offenders are included in a handbook that is accessible to all offenders and staff. When a literacy or communication problem exists, a staff member assists the offender.**

Comment:
None.

SELF-EVALUATION Agency Personnel	STANDARDS COMPLIANCE AUDIT Visiting Committee
Staff Signature(s): _____ _____ ❑ Compliance (list documentation) ❑ Noncompliance (see plan of action) ❑ Not applicable (justification attached) ❑ Plan of action waiver requested (justification attached) Prepare one of the following, as appropriate: 1) List documentation to support compliance; 2) Explain nonapplicability of standard: 3) Explain plan of action waiver request.	Auditor Signature(s): _____ _____ ❑ Compliance ❑ POA acceptable ❑ Noncompliance ❑ POA unacceptable ❑ Not Applicable ❑ Waiver acceptable ❑ Waiver unacceptable List deficiencies if standard is in noncompliance: **NOTE: List all deficiencies if standard is in noncompliance or not applicable. State exactly why standard is in noncompliance. Make complete comments in space above and attach any other information, if necessary. BE VERY SPECIFIC!**

Disciplinary Procedures

1-EM-3C-03   **Written policy, procedure, and practice provide for written guidelines regarding disciplinary procedures that specify which violations require notification to the court, the referring agency, and/or other staff that is not part of the program, including timing of notification for the violation.**

Comment:
All applicable rules, infractions, and disciplinary procedures must be included in a handbook.

SELF-EVALUATION Agency Personnel	STANDARDS COMPLIANCE AUDIT Visiting Committee
Staff Signature(s): _____ _____	Auditor Signature(s): _____ _____
❑ Compliance (list documentation) ❑ Noncompliance (see plan of action) ❑ Not applicable (justification attached) ❑ Plan of action waiver requested (justification attached) Prepare one of the following, as appropriate: 1) List documentation to support compliance; 2) Explain nonapplicability of standard: 3) Explain plan of action waiver request.	❑ Compliance ❑ POA acceptable ❑ Noncompliance ❑ POA unacceptable ❑ Not Applicable ❑ Waiver acceptable ❑ Waiver unacceptable List deficiencies if standard is in noncompliance: **NOTE: List all deficiencies if standard is in noncompliance or not applicable. State exactly why standard is in noncompliance. Make complete comments in space above and attach any other information, if necessary. BE VERY SPECIFIC!**

1-EM-3C-04 Written policy, procedure, and practice specify how the offender is notified of the alleged violation and the sanctions applicable to the specific violation. The offender has an opportunity to make a statement and the right to a copy of the report. If the violation is not being referred to another authority where the offender will have an opportunity to contest the alleged facts, there are procedures whereby the offender can exercise the right to contest the facts alleged in the report and/or the sanction applied.

Comment:
None.

SELF-EVALUATION Agency Personnel	STANDARDS COMPLIANCE AUDIT Visiting Committee
Staff Signature(s): _____ _____	Auditor Signature(s): _____ _____

SELF-EVALUATION — Agency Personnel:

❑ Compliance (list documentation)
❑ Noncompliance (see plan of action)
❑ Not applicable (justification attached)
❑ Plan of action waiver requested (justification attached)

Prepare one of the following, as appropriate:

1) List documentation to support compliance;
2) Explain nonapplicability of standard:
3) Explain plan of action waiver request.

STANDARDS COMPLIANCE AUDIT — Visiting Committee:

❑ Compliance   ❑ POA acceptable
❑ Noncompliance   ❑ POA unacceptable
❑ Not Applicable   ❑ Waiver acceptable
                       ❑ Waiver unacceptable

List deficiencies if standard is in noncompliance:

NOTE: List all deficiencies if standard is in noncompliance or not applicable. State exactly why standard is in noncompliance. Make complete comments in space above and attach any other information, if necessary. BE VERY SPECIFIC!

Program Removal

1-EM-3C-05   **Written policy, procedure, and practice defines the authority and process by which the program administrator may remove an offender from the program.**

Comment:
None.

SELF-EVALUATION Agency Personnel	STANDARDS COMPLIANCE AUDIT Visiting Committee
Staff Signature(s): _____ _____ ❑ Compliance (list documentation) ❑ Noncompliance (see plan of action) ❑ Not applicable (justification attached) ❑ Plan of action waiver requested (justification attached) Prepare one of the following, as appropriate: 1) List documentation to support compliance; 2) Explain nonapplicability of standard: 3) Explain plan of action waiver request.	Auditor Signature(s): _____ _____ ❑ Compliance ❑ POA acceptable ❑ Noncompliance ❑ POA unacceptable ❑ Not Applicable ❑ Waiver acceptable ❑ Waiver unacceptable List deficiencies if standard is in noncompliance: **NOTE: List all deficiencies if standard is in noncompliance or not applicable. State exactly why standard is in noncompliance. Make complete comments in space above and attach any other information, if necessary. BE VERY SPECIFIC!**

Part Four
Program Services

Section A
Reception and Orientation

Principle: All offenders undergo a thorough screening and assessment at admission and receive a thorough orientation to the procedures, rules, programs, and services.

Admission

1-EM-4A-01 **Written policy, procedure, and practice govern the admission process and criteria for acceptance in the program.**

Comment:
The policies and procedures governing the admission process should include, but not be limited to: types of information to be gathered on all applicants before admission, criteria for acceptance, and procedures to be followed when accepting or not accepting referrals.

SELF-EVALUATION Agency Personnel	STANDARDS COMPLIANCE AUDIT Visiting Committee
Staff Signature(s):	Auditor Signature(s):
❑ Compliance (list documentation) ❑ Noncompliance (see plan of action) ❑ Not applicable (justification attached) ❑ Plan of action waiver requested (justification attached) Prepare one of the following, as appropriate: 1) List documentation to support compliance; 2) Explain nonapplicability of standard: 3) Explain plan of action waiver request.	❑ Compliance ❑ POA acceptable ❑ Noncompliance ❑ POA unacceptable ❑ Not Applicable ❑ Waiver acceptable ❑ Waiver unacceptable List deficiencies if standard is in noncompliance: NOTE: List all deficiencies if standard is in noncompliance or not applicable. State exactly why standard is in noncompliance. Make complete comments in space above and attach any other information, if necessary. BE VERY SPECIFIC!

1-EM-4A-02 **Legal commitment authority is documented by court order, statute, or compact.**

Comment:
Regardless of the reason for commitment to the program, each offender's file should contain evidence of legal commitment.

SELF-EVALUATION Agency Personnel	STANDARDS COMPLIANCE AUDIT Visiting Committee
Staff Signature(s):	Auditor Signature(s):

Self-Evaluation:
- ❑ Compliance (list documentation)
- ❑ Noncompliance (see plan of action)
- ❑ Not applicable (justification attached)
- ❑ Plan of action waiver requested (justification attached)

Prepare one of the following, as appropriate:

1) List documentation to support compliance;
2) Explain nonapplicability of standard:
3) Explain plan of action waiver request.

Standards Compliance Audit:
- ❑ Compliance
- ❑ Noncompliance
- ❑ Not Applicable
- ❑ POA acceptable
- ❑ POA unacceptable
- ❑ Waiver acceptable
- ❑ Waiver unacceptable

List deficiencies if standard is in noncompliance:

NOTE: List all deficiencies if standard is in noncompliance or not applicable. State exactly why standard is in noncompliance. Make complete comments in space above and attach any other information, if necessary. BE VERY SPECIFIC!

Access to Programs and Services

1-EM-4A-03   **Written policy, procedure, and practice provide that program access and administrative decisions are made without regard to offenders' race, religion, national origin, sex, disability, or political views.**

Comment:
Offenders should be assured equal opportunities to participate in all programs.

SELF-EVALUATION Agency Personnel	STANDARDS COMPLIANCE AUDIT Visiting Committee
Staff Signature(s):	Auditor Signature(s):
_____ _____	_____ _____
❑ Compliance (list documentation) ❑ Noncompliance (see plan of action) ❑ Not applicable (justification attached) ❑ Plan of action waiver requested (justification attached) Prepare one of the following, as appropriate: 1) List documentation to support compliance; 2) Explain nonapplicability of standard: 3) Explain plan of action waiver request.	❑ Compliance ❑ POA acceptable ❑ Noncompliance ❑ POA unacceptable ❑ Not Applicable ❑ Waiver acceptable ❑ Waiver unacceptable List deficiencies if standard is in noncompliance: NOTE: List all deficiencies if standard is in noncompliance or not applicable. State exactly why standard is in noncompliance. Make complete comments in space above and attach any other information, if necessary. BE VERY SPECIFIC!

1-EM-4A-04   **Written policy, procedure, and practice provide that male and female offenders have equal access to the program and its activities.**

Comment:
None.

SELF-EVALUATION Agency Personnel	STANDARDS COMPLIANCE AUDIT Visiting Committee
Staff Signature(s): _____ _____ ❑ Compliance (list documentation) ❑ Noncompliance (see plan of action) ❑ Not applicable (justification attached) ❑ Plan of action waiver requested (justification attached) Prepare one of the following, as appropriate: 1) List documentation to support compliance; 2) Explain nonapplicability of standard: 3) Explain plan of action waiver request.	Auditor Signature(s): _____ _____ ❑ Compliance ❑ POA acceptable ❑ Noncompliance ❑ POA unacceptable ❑ Not Applicable ❑ Waiver acceptable ❑ Waiver unacceptable List deficiencies if standard is in noncompliance: **NOTE: List all deficiencies if standard is in noncompliance or not applicable. State exactly why standard is in noncompliance. Make complete comments in space above and attach any other information, if necessary. BE VERY SPECIFIC!**

Program Denial

1-EM-4A-05   **Written policy, procedure, and practice provide that the program advises the referring program when a prospective offender is not accepted into the program, stating specific reasons.**

Comment:
An important part of the referral process is the follow-up provided to the referring source. Such communication will assist the referring source in making future referrals.

SELF-EVALUATION Agency Personnel	STANDARDS COMPLIANCE AUDIT Visiting Committee
Staff Signature(s): _____ _____ ❑ Compliance (list documentation) ❑ Noncompliance (see plan of action) ❑ Not applicable (justification attached) ❑ Plan of action waiver requested (justification attached) Prepare one of the following, as appropriate: 1) List documentation to support compliance; 2) Explain nonapplicability of standard: 3) Explain plan of action waiver request.	Auditor Signature(s): _____ _____ ❑ Compliance ❑ POA acceptable ❑ Noncompliance ❑ POA unacceptable ❑ Not Applicable ❑ Waiver acceptable ❑ Waiver unacceptable List deficiencies if standard is in noncompliance: **NOTE: List all deficiencies if standard is in noncompliance or not applicable. State exactly why standard is in noncompliance. Make complete comments in space above and attach any other information, if necessary. BE VERY SPECIFIC!**

Admission Records

1-EM-4A-06   **The program records information on each offender to be admitted that includes, at a minimum, the following:**

- **name**
- **address**
- **social security number**
- **date of birth**
- **sex**
- **race or ethnic origin**
- **reason for referral**
- **who to notify in case of emergency**
- **date information gathered**
- **name of referring agency or committing authority**
- **social history, where available**
- **employer's name, address, and phone number, if any**
- **special medical problems or needs**
- **substance abuse history, if any**
- **personal physician, if applicable**
- **legal status, including jurisdiction, length, and conditions of placement**
- **signature of both interviewee and employee gathering information**

Comment:
The program's admission information form should include the basic data necessary to facilitate a continuous program for the offender. The information on the form is preliminary and can be expanded to meet the needs of individual facilities.

SELF-EVALUATION Agency Personnel	STANDARDS COMPLIANCE AUDIT Visiting Committee
Staff Signature(s): _____ _____	Auditor Signature(s): _____ _____
❏ Compliance (list documentation) ❏ Noncompliance (see plan of action) ❏ Not applicable (justification attached) ❏ Plan of action waiver requested (justification attached) Prepare one of the following, as appropriate: 1) List documentation to support compliance; 2) Explain nonapplicability of standard: 3) Explain plan of action waiver request.	❏ Compliance ❏ POA acceptable ❏ Noncompliance ❏ POA unacceptable ❏ Not Applicable ❏ Waiver acceptable ❏ Waiver unacceptable List deficiencies if standard is in noncompliance: NOTE: List all deficiencies if standard is in noncompliance or not applicable. State exactly why standard is in noncompliance. Make complete comments in space above and attach any other information, if necessary. BE VERY SPECIFIC!

Reception and Orientation

1-EM-4A-07   **Written policy, procedure, and practice provide that at the time of admission, program staff discuss with the offender program goals, service(s) available, rules governing conduct, and program rules; this is documented by employee and offender signatures.**

Comment:

It is important that offenders, at the time of admission, understand what can be expected of the program and what the program expects from them. This discussion can occur before admission and acceptance into the program. The discussion or orientation also should include, but not be limited to: curfew, program participation, rules, eligibility criteria for discharge, and staff expectations.

SELF-EVALUATION Agency Personnel	STANDARDS COMPLIANCE AUDIT Visiting Committee
Staff Signature(s):	Auditor Signature(s):
_____ _____ ❑ Compliance (list documentation) ❑ Noncompliance (see plan of action) ❑ Not applicable (justification attached) ❑ Plan of action waiver requested (justification attached) Prepare one of the following, as appropriate: 1) List documentation to support compliance; 2) Explain nonapplicability of standard: 3) Explain plan of action waiver request.	_____ _____ ❑ Compliance ❑ POA acceptable ❑ Noncompliance ❑ POA unacceptable ❑ Not Applicable ❑ Waiver acceptable ❑ Waiver unacceptable List deficiencies if standard is in noncompliance: **NOTE: List all deficiencies if standard is in noncompliance or not applicable. State exactly why standard is in noncompliance. Make complete comments in space above and attach any other information, if necessary. BE VERY SPECIFIC!**

1-EM-4A-08   **Written policy, procedure, and practice provide that offenders receive program orientation on or before the first day of program participation. Completion of orientation is documented by a statement signed and dated by the offender.**

Comment:
At the time of orientation, the offender reads, discusses, and signs written statements and receives a copy of program rules, regulations, disciplinary procedures, and all program guidelines including available services and goals. Parents/guardians of juvenile offenders obtain the same information at the same time. All members living in the household should receive orientation.

SELF-EVALUATION Agency Personnel	STANDARDS COMPLIANCE AUDIT Visiting Committee
Staff Signature(s): _____ _____ ❑ Compliance (list documentation) ❑ Noncompliance (see plan of action) ❑ Not applicable (justification attached) ❑ Plan of action waiver requested (justification attached) Prepare one of the following, as appropriate: 1) List documentation to support compliance; 2) Explain nonapplicability of standard: 3) Explain plan of action waiver request.	Auditor Signature(s): _____ _____ ❑ Compliance ❑ POA acceptable ❑ Noncompliance ❑ POA unacceptable ❑ Not Applicable ❑ Waiver acceptable ❑ Waiver unacceptable List deficiencies if standard is in noncompliance: **NOTE: List all deficiencies if standard is in noncompliance or not applicable. State exactly why standard is in noncompliance. Make complete comments in space above and attach any other information, if necessary. BE VERY SPECIFIC!**

1-EM-4A-09   **Written policy, procedure, and practice provide that new offenders receive written orientation materials and/or translations in their own language. When a literacy problem exists, a staff member assists the offender in understanding the material. Completion of orientation is documented by a statement signed and dated by the offender.**

Comment:
Orientation should include informal classes, distribution of written materials about the programs, program's rules and regulations, and discussions. Orientation also should be used to observe offender behavior and to identify special problems.

SELF-EVALUATION Agency Personnel	STANDARDS COMPLIANCE AUDIT Visiting Committee
Staff Signature(s): _____ _____ ❑ Compliance (list documentation) ❑ Noncompliance (see plan of action) ❑ Not applicable (justification attached) ❑ Plan of action waiver requested (justification attached) Prepare one of the following, as appropriate: 1) List documentation to support compliance; 2) Explain nonapplicability of standard: 3) Explain plan of action waiver request.	Auditor Signature(s): _____ _____ ❑ Compliance ❑ POA acceptable ❑ Noncompliance ❑ POA unacceptable ❑ Not Applicable ❑ Waiver acceptable ❑ Waiver unacceptable List deficiencies if standard is in noncompliance: **NOTE: List all deficiencies if standard is in noncompliance or not applicable. State exactly why standard is in noncompliance. Make complete comments in space above and attach any other information, if necessary. BE VERY SPECIFIC!**

Program Fee Collection

1-EM-4A-10 **Written policy, procedure, and practice provide that if fees are collected, there is documentation that the offender has been informed of the policies and procedures regarding nonpayment of fees.**

Comment:
None.

SELF-EVALUATION Agency Personnel	STANDARDS COMPLIANCE AUDIT Visiting Committee
Staff Signature(s): _____ _____ ❑ Compliance (list documentation) ❑ Noncompliance (see plan of action) ❑ Not applicable (justification attached) ❑ Plan of action waiver requested (justification attached) Prepare one of the following, as appropriate: 1) List documentation to support compliance; 2) Explain nonapplicability of standard: 3) Explain plan of action waiver request.	Auditor Signature(s): _____ _____ ❑ Compliance ❑ POA acceptable ❑ Noncompliance ❑ POA unacceptable ❑ Not Applicable ❑ Waiver acceptable ❑ Waiver unacceptable List deficiencies if standard is in noncompliance: **NOTE: List all deficiencies if standard is in noncompliance or not applicable. State exactly why standard is in noncompliance. Make complete comments in space above and attach any other information, if necessary. BE VERY SPECIFIC!**

1-EM-4A-11   **Written policy, procedure, and practice provide for those who are unable to pay program costs and/or the cost of telephone service.**

Comment:
No one is refused program services because of the inability to pay costs.

SELF-EVALUATION Agency Personnel	STANDARDS COMPLIANCE AUDIT Visiting Committee
Staff Signature(s): _____ _____ ❑ Compliance (list documentation) ❑ Noncompliance (see plan of action) ❑ Not applicable (justification attached) ❑ Plan of action waiver requested (justification attached) Prepare one of the following, as appropriate: 1) List documentation to support compliance; 2) Explain nonapplicability of standard: 3) Explain plan of action waiver request.	Auditor Signature(s): _____ _____ ❑ Compliance ❑ POA acceptable ❑ Noncompliance ❑ POA unacceptable ❑ Not Applicable ❑ Waiver acceptable ❑ Waiver unacceptable List deficiencies if standard is in noncompliance: **NOTE: List all deficiencies if standard is in noncompliance or not applicable. State exactly why standard is in noncompliance. Make complete comments in space above and attach any other information, if necessary. BE VERY SPECIFIC!**

Section B
Classification

Principle: Offenders are classified to the most appropriate level of custody and programming, both on admission and on review of their status.

Program Plan

1-EM-4B-01   **Written policy, procedure, and practice provide that program staff complete an individualized plan for each offender within one week of the installation of any personal monitoring device.**

Comment:
None.

SELF-EVALUATION Agency Personnel	STANDARDS COMPLIANCE AUDIT Visiting Committee
Staff Signature(s):	Auditor Signature(s):
_____	_____
_____	_____
❑ Compliance (list documentation) ❑ Noncompliance (see plan of action) ❑ Not applicable (justification attached) ❑ Plan of action waiver requested (justification attached) Prepare one of the following, as appropriate: 1) List documentation to support compliance; 2) Explain nonapplicability of standard: 3) Explain plan of action waiver request.	❑ Compliance ❑ POA acceptable ❑ Noncompliance ❑ POA unacceptable ❑ Not Applicable ❑ Waiver acceptable ❑ Waiver unacceptable List deficiencies if standard is in noncompliance: NOTE: List all deficiencies if standard is in noncompliance or not applicable. State exactly why standard is in noncompliance. Make complete comments in space above and attach any other information, if necessary. BE VERY SPECIFIC!

1-EM-4B-02   **In accordance with the requirements of the authority having jurisdiction, written policy, procedure, and practice provide that a detailed written offender schedule is developed and signed by a staff member and the offender.**

Comment:
None.

SELF-EVALUATION Agency Personnel	STANDARDS COMPLIANCE AUDIT Visiting Committee
Staff Signature(s): _____ _____ ❑ Compliance (list documentation) ❑ Noncompliance (see plan of action) ❑ Not applicable (justification attached) ❑ Plan of action waiver requested (justification attached) Prepare one of the following, as appropriate: 1) List documentation to support compliance; 2) Explain nonapplicability of standard: 3) Explain plan of action waiver request.	Auditor Signature(s): _____ _____ ❑ Compliance ❑ POA acceptable ❑ Noncompliance ❑ POA unacceptable ❑ Not Applicable ❑ Waiver acceptable ❑ Waiver unacceptable List deficiencies if standard is in noncompliance: **NOTE: List all deficiencies if standard is in noncompliance or not applicable. State exactly why standard is in noncompliance. Make complete comments in space above and attach any other information, if necessary. BE VERY SPECIFIC!**

1-EM-4B-03   **Written policy, procedure, and practice provide that offenders have input into planning, problem solving, and decision making related to their participation in the program.**

Comment:
Provisions should be made for offenders to take part in program planning and any decisions to be made that may affect the offenders' lives. Such participation enables offenders to assume responsibility, develop decision-making skills, and identify more closely with the program.

SELF-EVALUATION Agency Personnel	STANDARDS COMPLIANCE AUDIT Visiting Committee
Staff Signature(s): _____ _____	Auditor Signature(s): _____ _____

Staff Signature(s):

_____

_____

❑ Compliance (list documentation)
❑ Noncompliance (see plan of action)
❑ Not applicable (justification attached)
❑ Plan of action waiver requested (justification attached)

Prepare one of the following, as appropriate:

1) List documentation to support compliance;
2) Explain nonapplicability of standard:
3) Explain plan of action waiver request.

Auditor Signature(s):

_____

_____

❑ Compliance   ❑ POA acceptable
❑ Noncompliance   ❑ POA unacceptable
❑ Not Applicable   ❑ Waiver acceptable
                              ❑ Waiver unacceptable

List deficiencies if standard is in noncompliance:

NOTE: List all deficiencies if standard is in noncompliance or not applicable. State exactly why standard is in noncompliance. Make complete comments in space above and attach any other information, if necessary. BE VERY SPECIFIC!

Offender Reports

1-EM-4B-04   **Written policy, procedure, and practice require that staff make systematic reviews of each offender's progress in the program at least monthly and advise the offender of the documented review. The offender must sign the document acknowledging its review.**

Comment:
None.

SELF-EVALUATION Agency Personnel	STANDARDS COMPLIANCE AUDIT Visiting Committee
Staff Signature(s):	Auditor Signature(s):
_____	_____
_____	_____

SELF-EVALUATION:

❑ Compliance (list documentation)
❑ Noncompliance (see plan of action)
❑ Not applicable (justification attached)
❑ Plan of action waiver requested (justification attached)

Prepare one of the following, as appropriate:

1) List documentation to support compliance;
2) Explain nonapplicability of standard:
3) Explain plan of action waiver request.

STANDARDS COMPLIANCE AUDIT:

❑ Compliance   ❑ POA acceptable
❑ Noncompliance   ❑ POA unacceptable
❑ Not Applicable   ❑ Waiver acceptable
                      ❑ Waiver unacceptable

List deficiencies if standard is in noncompliance:

NOTE: List all deficiencies if standard is in noncompliance or not applicable. State exactly why standard is in noncompliance. Make complete comments in space above and attach any other information, if necessary. BE VERY SPECIFIC!

1-EM-4B-05   **Written policy, procedure, and practice provide that the offender's progress reports are available to committing and/or referring authorities at least quarterly or in accordance with the authority having jurisdiction.**

Comment:
None.

SELF-EVALUATION Agency Personnel	STANDARDS COMPLIANCE AUDIT Visiting Committee
Staff Signature(s): _____ _____ ❑ Compliance (list documentation) ❑ Noncompliance (see plan of action) ❑ Not applicable (justification attached) ❑ Plan of action waiver requested (justification attached) Prepare one of the following, as appropriate: 1) List documentation to support compliance; 2) Explain nonapplicability of standard: 3) Explain plan of action waiver request.	Auditor Signature(s): _____ _____ ❑ Compliance ❑ POA acceptable ❑ Noncompliance ❑ POA unacceptable ❑ Not Applicable ❑ Waiver acceptable ❑ Waiver unacceptable List deficiencies if standard is in noncompliance: **NOTE: List all deficiencies if standard is in noncompliance or not applicable. State exactly why standard is in noncompliance. Make complete comments in space above and attach any other information, if necessary. BE VERY SPECIFIC!**

Services and Referrals

1-EM-4B-06   **The program provides comprehensive case management services and referrals based on individual needs.**

Comment:
None.

SELF-EVALUATION Agency Personnel	STANDARDS COMPLIANCE AUDIT Visiting Committee
Staff Signature(s): _____ _____	Auditor Signature(s): _____ _____

Self-Evaluation:
- ❑ Compliance (list documentation)
- ❑ Noncompliance (see plan of action)
- ❑ Not applicable (justification attached)
- ❑ Plan of action waiver requested (justification attached)

Prepare one of the following, as appropriate:

1) List documentation to support compliance;
2) Explain nonapplicability of standard:
3) Explain plan of action waiver request.

Standards Compliance Audit:
- ❑ Compliance
- ❑ Noncompliance
- ❑ Not Applicable
- ❑ POA acceptable
- ❑ POA unacceptable
- ❑ Waiver acceptable
- ❑ Waiver unacceptable

List deficiencies if standard is in noncompliance:

NOTE: List all deficiencies if standard is in noncompliance or not applicable. State exactly why standard is in noncompliance. Make complete comments in space above and attach any other information, if necessary. BE VERY SPECIFIC!

Section C
Release

Principle: A program is provided to offenders to assist them in their transition to the community.

Release Report

1-EM-4C-01   **A report is prepared at the termination of program participation that reviews the offender's performance. This report shall include, at a minimum:**

- **a summary of the offenders' program activities**
- **any unusual occurrences**
- **community resource references that affected the outcome of supervision**
- **staff assessment of the offender's program participation**

A copy of the report is maintained in the offender's case record and referred to the appropriate authorities.

Comment:
None.

SELF-EVALUATION Agency Personnel	STANDARDS COMPLIANCE AUDIT Visiting Committee
Staff Signature(s): _____ _____ ❑ Compliance (list documentation) ❑ Noncompliance (see plan of action) ❑ Not applicable (justification attached) ❑ Plan of action waiver requested (justification attached) Prepare one of the following, as appropriate: 1) List documentation to support compliance; 2) Explain nonapplicability of standard: 3) Explain plan of action waiver request.	Auditor Signature(s): _____ _____ ❑ Compliance ❑ POA acceptable ❑ Noncompliance ❑ POA unacceptable ❑ Not Applicable ❑ Waiver acceptable ❑ Waiver unacceptable List deficiencies if standard is in noncompliance: **NOTE: List all deficiencies if standard is in noncompliance or not applicable. State exactly why standard is in noncompliance. Make complete comments in space above and attach any other information, if necessary. BE VERY SPECIFIC!**

Final Release

1-EM-4C-02   **Written procedures for releasing offenders at the end of their term include, but are not limited to, the following:**

- **verification of identity**
- **verification of release papers**
- **completion of release arrangements, including notification of the parole authorities in the jurisdiction of release, if required**

Comment:
The release process should ensure that all matters relating to the program are completed. If released to another agency or program, the procedures regarding the transfer should include the forwarding of records.

SELF-EVALUATION Agency Personnel	STANDARDS COMPLIANCE AUDIT Visiting Committee
Staff Signature(s):	Auditor Signature(s):
❏ Compliance (list documentation) ❏ Noncompliance (see plan of action) ❏ Not applicable (justification attached) ❏ Plan of action waiver requested (justification attached) Prepare one of the following, as appropriate: 1) List documentation to support compliance; 2) Explain nonapplicability of standard: 3) Explain plan of action waiver request.	❏ Compliance ❏ POA acceptable ❏ Noncompliance ❏ POA unacceptable ❏ Not Applicable ❏ Waiver acceptable ❏ Waiver unacceptable List deficiencies if standard is in noncompliance: **NOTE: List all deficiencies if standard is in noncompliance or not applicable. State exactly why standard is in noncompliance. Make complete comments in space above and attach any other information, if necessary. BE VERY SPECIFIC!**

Appendix A
Guidelines for Contracting for Electronic Monitoring Services

This appendix refers to and is applicable only to those agencies that have a contract or agreement for monitoring services. The term contract, as used in this section, refers to a legal document or an agreement. Typical contracts are broken down into three sections: equipment description, monitoring activities, and field service. This information is provided for informational purposes and is in response to frequent inquiry concerning contracts. Each contract should be reviewed and discussed with legal counsel.

Equipment Information

1. Contains a statement of the goals, objectives, and mission of the program in which the equipment is to be used so that the required equipment is compatible with these statements.

2. Requires safe and effective equipment, specifying minimal acceptable standards.

3. Defines when improved equipment will replace present equipment.

4. Specifies timeframes, shipping schedules, and costs for equipment that is lost, damaged, stolen, or rendered inoperable, even if the offender is ultimately held responsible for such costs.

5. Designates timeframes and shipping schedules to maintain an inventory of spare parts and equipment as a function of the number of units presently in use (for example, a contract could require two spare units when one to 25 units are in use and one spare for every 25 units in use thereafter).

6. Provides for on-site training for staff in the installation and use of the equipment, data requirements, and the provision of written training materials for use with staff and offenders.

7. Specifies the liability and indemnification of the vendor and the contracting entity in the event of legal action.

8. Specifies the insurance that the vendor is required to maintain.

9. Allows for termination of the contract if (a) either party is not abiding by the terms of the contract, or (b) if the entity loses its funding, including the timeframe and what is to be done with the equipment.

10. Specifies emergency equipment, including backup plans of electronic data.

Monitoring Activities

1. How referrals are to be made and the conditions under which a case will be accepted or rejected.

2. How offenders are to be removed for disciplinary reasons.

3. The procedures to be followed in the cases of any emergency, specifically including loss of telephone service or electric power by the vendor or by the offender and computer failures.

4. The expected extent of coverage (e.g., 24 hours per day), the reporting timeframes for various events, and actions to be taken.

5. The data required for the operation of the service including sources of that data, how it is obtained, and how it is input into the system.

6. The procedures for establishing the offender's initial schedule and for modifying the schedule, while ensuring that only the designated authorized staff can modify the schedule.

7. Designate expected office and equipment security requirements.

Field Services

1. The number of documented face-to-face offender visits that will occur in given time periods in the office and in the field.

2. Contractor responsibilities for contractor-provided and/or referral to community resources for services, such as counseling, job placement, AA, parenting, etc.

3. How services and community activities are reported to referral sources.

4. Reporting requirements, including the expectation on timeframes, nature and content of reports, as well as to whom the reports are being sent.

5. Determination of fee amounts, fee collection schedule, procedures for waivers, reporting, and accounting.

6. Requirements for case files.

7. Required staffing/client ratios.

Appendix B
Definition of "Qualified Individual" for Safety and Sanitation Inspections

Several standards refer to documentation and inspections by "qualified individuals." (For example, Safety and Emergency Procedures standards.) Such persons may also be referred to as "independent, qualified source," "qualified departmental staff member," "qualified designee," or "qualified fire and safety officer."

A "qualified individual" is a person whose training, education, and/or experience specifically qualifies him or her to do the job indicated in the standard.

I. General Requirements

When a standard calls for inspections, the individual conducting them needs to be trained in the application of appropriate codes and regulations. Standards do not specify the number of hours of training required, as this is determined in part by the tasks assigned. At a minimum, though, the qualified individual must (1) be familiar with the applicable codes and regulations and their requirements; (2) be able to use the appropriate instruments for measuring and documenting code compliance; (3) be able to complete checklists and prepare the necessary reports; and (4) have the authority to make corrections when deficiencies are found.

Training is often obtained from code officials or inspectors (fire marshals, building officials); government agencies that have statutory authority for inspections in a particular area (health department, labor department); or private organizations, such as the National Fire Protection Association. Often the individual obtains written certification or approval from these authorities to conduct in-house inspections. When trained and certified by the above sources to do so, a central office specialist may train and assist facility staff to conduct inspections.

II. Specific Requirements

A. Authority Having Jurisdiction
The term "authority having jurisdiction" is defined as follows:

The authority having jurisdiction must be knowledgeable about the requirements of the National Fire Protection *Life Safety Code*. The authority having jurisdiction may be a federal, state, local, or other regional department or individual, such as the fire chief, fire marshal, chief of a fire prevention bureau, labor department, health department, building official, electrical inspector, or others with statutory authority. The authority having jurisdiction may be employed by the department/agency, provided that he or she is not under the authority of the facility administrator and that the report generated is referred to higher authorities within the department/agency independent of influence by the facility administrator or staff. This rule applies no matter who generates the report.

The definition also applies to the terms "independent, qualified source" and "independent, outside source."

B. Inspections
Qualified individuals conducting the inspections required in the standards may be facility staff members.

The qualified individual responsible for conducting *monthly* inspections (e.g., fire and safety officer, safety/sanitation specialist) may be a facility staff member trained in the application of jurisdictional codes and regulations. Periodically and as needed, this individual receives assistance from the independent authority or central office specialist(s) on requirements and inspections. This assistance may include participation in quarterly or biannual inspections. Training for the individual conducting the monthly inspections may be provided by the applicable agencies or through the agency's central office specialist(s).

The qualified departmental staff member who conducts *weekly* inspections of the facility may be a facility staff member who has received training in and is familiar with the safety and sanitation requirements of the jurisdiction. At a minimum, on-the-job training from the facility's safety/sanitation specialist or the fire and safety officer regarding applicable regulations is expected, including use of checklists and methods of documentation.

The periodic weekly and monthly inspections may be conducted by either a combination of qualified individuals or one specialist, as long as the schedules and minimum qualifications described above are met. Safety and sanitation inspections may be conducted by the same person, provided this individual is familiar with the regulations for both types of inspections. When safety and sanitation requirements differ substantially, it may sometimes be necessary to call on several qualified individuals to conduct the inspections required by the standards. Using more than one person is strongly recommended.

III. Compliance Audits

In conducting standards compliance audits, Commission Visiting Committees will review documentation submitted by the facilities to assist them in judging the qualifications of these individuals. In making compliance decisions, the audit teams will look closely at the facility's entire program—both practices and results—for ensuring safety and sanitation.

Appendix C
Guidelines for the Control and Use of
Flammable, Toxic, and Caustic Substances

This appendix provides definitions and recommendations to assist agencies in the application of standards that address the control of materials that present a hazard to staff and offenders.

Substances that do not contain any of the properties discussed in the guidelines but are labeled "Keep out of reach of children" or "May be harmful if swallowed" are not necessarily subject to the controls specified in the guidelines. Their use and control, however, including the quantities available, should be evaluated and addressed in agency policy. Questions concerning the use and control of any substance should be resolved by examining the manufacturer's Material Safety Data Sheet.

I. Definitions

Flash point—The minimum temperature at which a liquid will give off sufficient vapors to form an ignitable mixture with the air near the surface of the liquid (or in the vessel used).

Flammable liquid—A substance with a flash point below 100° Fahrenheit (37.8 degrees Centigrade). Classified by flash point as a Class I liquid. (See Table A.)

Combustible liquid—A substance with a flash point at or above 100° Fahrenheit. Classified by flash point as a Class II or Class III liquid. (See Table A.)

Toxic material—A substance that, through chemical reaction or mixture, can produce possible injury or harm to the body by entry through the skin, digestive tract, or respiratory tract. The toxicity is dependent on the quantity absorbed and the rate, method, and site of absorption. (See Table A.)

Caustic material—A substance capable of destroying or eating away by chemical reaction. (See Table A.)

It is possible that a substance may possess more than one of the above properties; therefore the safety requirements for all applicable properties should be considered.

II. General Guidelines

A. Issuance
All flammable, caustic, and toxic substances should be issued (e.g., drawn from supply points to canisters or dispensed) only under the supervision of authorized staff.

B. Amounts
All such substances should be issued only in the amount necessary for one day's needs.

C. Supervision
All persons using such substances should be closely supervised by qualified staff.

D. Accountability
All such substances must be accounted for before, during, and after their use.

Table A
Common Flammable, Toxic, and Caustic Substances

Class I Liquids
  Gasoline
  Benzine (Petroleum ether)
  Acetone
  Hexane
  Lacquer
  Lacquer thinner
  Denatured alcohol
  Ethyl alcohol
  Xylene (Xylol)
  Contact cement (flammable)
  Toludi (Toluene)
  Methyl ethyl ether
  Methyl ethyl ketone
  Naphtha Y, M, and P

Class II Liquids
  Diesel fuel
  Motor oil
  Kerosene
  Cleaning solvents
  Mineral spirits
  Agitene

Class III Liquids
  Paints (oil base)
  Linseed oil
  Mineral oil
  Neatsfoot oil
  Sunray conditioner
  Guardian fluid

Toxic Substances
  Ammonia
  Chlorine
  Antifreeze
  Duplicating fluid
  Methyl alcohol (Wood alcohol or Methanol)
  Defoliants
  Herbicides
  Pesticides
  Rodenticides

Caustic Substances
  Lye
  Muriatic acid
  Caustic soda
  Sulfuric acid
  Tannic acid

III. Specific Guidelines for Storage, Use, and Disposal

A. Flammable and Combustible Liquids
Any liquid or aerosol that is required to be labeled "flammable" or "combustible" under the Federal Hazardous Substances Labeling Act must be stored and used according to label recommendations and in a way that does not endanger life and property.

1. Storage
Lighting fixtures and electrical equipment in flammable liquid storage rooms must conform to the *National Electrical Code* requirements for installation in hazardous locations.

Storage rooms must meet the following specifications:

- be of fire-resistant construction and properly secured

- have self-closing fire doors at all openings

- have either a four-inch sill or a four-inch depressed floor (inside storage rooms only)

- have a ventilation system—either mechanical or gravity flow within twelve inches of the floor—that provides at least six air changes per hour in the room

---

Each storage cabinet must be

- properly constructed and securely locked

- conspicuously labeled "Flammable—Keep Fire Away"

- used to store no more than sixty gallons of Class I or Class II liquids or 120 gallons of Class III liquids

Storage rooms and cabinets must be properly secured and supervised by an authorized staff member any time they are in use. Doors and cabinets shall be placed so that they do not obstruct access to exits, stairways, and other areas normally used for evacuation in the event of fire or other emergency.

All portable containers for flammable and combustible liquids other than the original shipping containers must be approved safety cans listed or labeled by a nationally recognized testing laboratory. Containers should bear legible labels identifying the contents.

All excess liquids should remain in their original container in the storage room or cabinet. All containers should be tightly closed when not in use.

2. Use

The use of any flammable or combustible liquid must conform with the provisions and precautions listed in the manufacturer's Material Safety Data Sheet.

Flammable and combustible liquids can be dispensed only by an authorized staff member. The only acceptable methods for drawing from or transferring these liquids into containers inside a building are (1) through a closed piping system, (2) from safety cans, (3) by a device drawing through the top, or (4) by gravity through an approved self-closing system. An approved grounding and bonding system must be used when liquids are dispensed from drums.

Only liquids with a flash point at or above 100° Fahrenheit (e.g., Stoddard solvents, kerosene) can be used for cleaning. Such operations must be performed in an approved parts cleaner or dip-tank fitted with a fusible link lid with a 160° Fahrenheit melting-temperature link. *Under no circumstances may flammable liquids be used for cleaning.*

3. Disposal

Excess flammable or combustible liquids must be disposed of properly. The Material Safety Data Sheet for each substance prescribes the proper method of disposal and related precautions.

4. Spills

Information on the proper course of action for chemical spills is contained in the Material Safety Data Sheet for each substance.

B. Toxic and Caustic Substances

1. Storage

All toxic and caustic materials are to be stored in their original containers in a secure area in each department. The manufacturer's label must be kept intact on the container.

2. Use
Toxic and caustic substances can be drawn only by a staff member. The Material Safety Data Sheet for each substance details the necessary provisions and precautions for its use.

Unused portions are to be returned to the original container in the storage area or, if appropriate, stored in the storage area in a suitable, clearly labeled container.

3. Disposal
See disposal guidelines for Flammable and Combustible Liquids above.

4. Spills
See spills guidelines for Flammable and Combustible Liquids above.

C. Poisonous Substances
Poisonous substances or chemicals are those that pose a very high (Class I) caustic hazard due to their toxicity. Examples: methyl alcohol, sulfuric acid, muriatic acid, caustic soda, tannic acid. There are special precautions on the control and use of methyl alcohol (also known as wood alcohol or methanol), which is a flammable, poisonous liquid commonly used in industrial applications (e.g., shellac thinner, paint solvent, duplicating fluid, solvents for leather cements and dyes, flushing fluid for hydraulic brake systems). *Drinking methyl alcohol can cause death or permanent blindness.*

The use of any product containing methyl alcohol must be directly supervised by staff. Products containing methyl alcohol in a diluted state, such as shoe dye, may be issued to inmates or residents, but only in the smallest workable quantities.

Immediate medical attention is imperative whenever methyl alcohol poisoning is suspected.

D. Other Toxic Substances

1. Permanent antifreeze containing ethylene glycol should be stored in a locked area and dispensed only by authorized staff.

2. Typewriter cleaner containing carbon tetrachloride or tricholorochane should be dispensed in small quantities and used under direct supervision.

3. The use of cleaning fluid containing carbon tetrachloride or tetrachloride or tricholoroethylene must be strictly controlled.

4. Glues of all types may contain hazardous chemicals and should receive close attention at every stage of handling. Nontoxic products should be used when possible. Toxic glues must be stored under lock and used under close supervision.

5. The use of dyes and cements for leather requires close supervision. Nonflammable types should be used whenever possible.

6. Ethyl alcohol, isopropyl alcohol, and other antiseptic products should be stored and used only in the medical department. The use of such chemicals must be closely supervised. Whenever possible, such chemicals should be diluted and issued only in small quantities so as to prevent any injurious or lethal accumulation.

7. Pesticides contain many types of poisons. The staff member with responsibility for the facility's safety program should be responsible for purchasing, storing, and dispensing any pesticide. All pesticides should be stored under lock. NOTE: Only chemicals approved by the Environmental Protection Agency shall be used. DDT and 1080 (sodium fluoracetate) are among those chemicals absolutely prohibited.

8. Herbicides must be stored under lock. The staff member responsible for herbicides must have a current state license as a Certified Private Applicator. Proper clothing and protective gear must be used when applying herbicides.

9. Lyes must be used only in dye solutions and only under the direct supervision of staff.

IV. Responsibilities

A. Inventories
Constant inventories should be maintained for all flammable, toxic, and caustic substances used and stored in each department. A bin record card should be maintained for each such substance to accurately reflect acquisitions, disbursements, and the amounts on hand.

B. Departmental Files
Each department using any flammable, toxic, or caustic substance should maintain a file of the manufacturer's Material Safety Data Sheet for each substance. This file should be updated at least annually. The file should also contain a list of all areas where these substances are stored, along with a plant diagram and legend. A copy of all information in the file, including the Material Safety Data Sheets, should be supplied to the staff member responsible for the facility's safety program.

C. Master Index
The person responsible for the facility's safety program should compile a master index of all flammable, caustic, and toxic substances in the facility, including their locations and Material Safety Data Sheets. This information should be kept in the safety office (or comparable location) and should be supplied to the local fire department. The master index should also contain an up-to-date list of emergency phone numbers (e.g., local fire department, local poison control center).

D. Personal Responsibility
It is the responsibility of each person using these substances to follow all prescribed safety precautions, wear personal protective equipment when necessary, and report all hazards or spills to the proper authority. The protection of life, property, and the environment depends on it.

Glossary

Absconder — An offender who fails to report for probation or aftercare supervision or an escapee or runaway.

Adjudicatory hearing — A hearing to determine whether the allegations of a petition are supported by the evidence beyond a reasonable doubt or by the preponderance of the evidence.

Administrative segregation — A form of separation from the general population administered by the classification committee or other authorized group when the continued presence of the inmate in the general population would pose a serious threat to life, property, self, staff, or other inmates or to the security or orderly running of the institution. Inmates pending investigation for trial on a criminal act or pending transfer also can be included. (See *Protective custody* and *Segregation*.)

Administrator of field services — The individual directly responsible for directing and controlling the operations of the adult probation and/or parole field services program. This person may be a division head in a large correctional agency, a chief probation officer answering to a judge, or the administrative officer of a court or parole authority with responsibility for the field services program.

Admission — The process of entry into a program. During admission processing, the juvenile or adult offender receives an orientation to program goals, rules, and regulations. Assignment to living quarters and to appropriate staff also is completed at this time.

Adult community residential service — Also referred to as halfway house, a community-based program providing group residence (such as a house, work release center, prerelease center) for probationers, parolees, residents in incarcerated status, and referrals through the courts or other agencies. Clients also may receive these services from the agency on a nonresidential basis. (See *Out-client*.)

Adult correctional institution — A confinement facility, usually under state or federal auspices, that has custodial authority over adults sentenced to confinement for more than one year.

Adult detention facility **or** *Jail* — A local confinement facility with temporary custodial authority. Adults can be confined pending adjudication for 48 hours or more and usually for sentences of up to two years.

Affirmative action — A concept designed to ensure equal opportunity for all persons regardless of race, religion, age, sex, or ethnic origin. These equal opportunities include all personnel programming, such as selection, retention, rate of pay, demotion, transfer, layoff, termination, and promotion.

Aftercare — Control, supervision, and care exercised over juveniles released from facilities through a stated release program. (See *Releasing authority*.)

Agency — The unit of a governing authority that has direct responsibility for the operations of a corrections program, including the implementation of policy as set by the governing authority. For a community residential center, this would be the administrative headquarters of the facilities. A single community facility that is not a part of a formal consolidation of community facilities is considered to be an agency. In a public agency, this could be a probation department, welfare department, or similar agency. For a juvenile correctional organization, this would be the central office responsible for governing the juvenile correctional system for the jurisdiction.

Agency administrator — The administrative officer appointed by the governing authority or designee who is responsible for all operations of the agency, such as the department of corrections or parole, and all related programs under his or her control.

Agency industries administrator — The individual who has functional responsibility for industries operations throughout the correctional system. Titles, such as head of industries, superintendent, chief, director, or general manager, may be used to denote this position.

Alternative meal service — Special foods provided to comply with the medical, religious, or security requirements. Alternative meals must always be designed to ensure that basic health needs are met and are provided in strict compliance with the policies signed by the chief executive officer, the chief medical officer, and for the religious diets, by the appropriate religious leader.

Audit — An examination of agency or facility records or accounts to check their accuracy, which is conducted by a person or persons not directly involved in the creation and maintenance of these records or accounts. An independent audit results in an opinion that either affirms or disaffirms the accuracy of records or accounts. An operational or internal audit usually results in a report to management that is not shared with those outside the agency.

Booking — Both a law enforcement process and a detention facility procedure. As a police administrative action, it is an official recording of an arrest and the identification of the person, place, time, arresting authority, and reason for the arrest. In a detention facility, it is a procedure for the admission of a person charged with or convicted for an offense, which includes searching, fingerprinting, photographing, medical screening, and collecting personal history data. Booking also includes the inventory and storage of the individual's personal property.

Boot camp — A short-term correctional unit designed to combine elements of basic military training programs and appropriate correctional components.

Camp — A nonsecure residential program located in a relatively remote area. The residents participate in a structured program that emphasizes outdoor work, including conservation and related activities. There are often 20 to 60 residents in these facilities.

Career development plan — The planned sequence of promotions within an agency that contains provision for (1) vertical movement throughout the entire range of a particular discipline, (2) horizontal movement encouraging lateral and promotional movement between disciplines, and (3) opportunity for all to compete for the position of head of the agency. Progression along these three dimensions can occur as long as the candidate has the ambition, ability, and required qualifications.

Case conference — A conference between individuals working with the juvenile or adult offender to see that court-ordered services are being provided.

Casework — The function of the caseworker, social worker, or other professional in providing social services, such as counseling, to individuals in custody.

Cellblock — A group or cluster of single and/or multiple occupancy cells or detention rooms immediately adjacent and directly accessible to a day or activity room. In some facilities, the cellblock consists of a row of cells fronted by a dayroom of corridor-like proportions.

Chemical agent — An active substance, such as tear gas, used to defer activities that might cause personal injury or property damage.

Chief of police — A local law enforcement official who is the appointed or elected chief executive of a police department and is responsible for the operation of the city jail or lockup.

Chronic care — Health care provided to patients over a long period of time.

Classification — A process for determining the needs and requirements of those for whom confinement has been ordered and for assigning them to housing units and programs according to their needs and existing resources.

Co-correctional facility — An institution designed to house both male and female juvenile or adult offenders.

Code of ethics — A set of rules describing acceptable standards of conduct for all employees.

Committing authority — The agency or court responsible for placing a youth in a program.

Community resources — Human services agencies, service clubs, citizen interest groups, self-help groups, and individual citizen volunteers that offer services, facilities, or other functions that can meet the needs of the facility or have the potential to assist residents. These various resources, which may be public or private, national or local, may assist with material and financial support, guidance, counseling, and supportive services.

Contraband — Any item possessed by confined juvenile or adult offenders or found within the facility that is illegal by law or expressly prohibited by those legally charged with the administration and operation of the facility or program.

Contractor — A person or organization that agrees to furnish materials or to perform services for the facility or jurisdiction at a specified price. Contractors operating in correctional facilities are subject to all applicable rules and regulations for the facility.

Contractual arrangement — An agreement with a private party (such as an incorporated agency or married couple) to provide services to juvenile or adult offenders for compensation. (See *Independent operator*.)

Control center — A very secure, self-contained unit designed to maintain the security of the facility. Policies governing the design, staffing, and accessibility of the control center ensure that it cannot be commandeered by unauthorized persons.

Corporal punishment — Any act of inflicting punishment directly on the body, causing pain or injury.

Correctional facility — A facility used for the incarceration of individuals accused or convicted of criminal activity. A correctional facility is managed by a single chief executive officer with broad authority for the operation of the facility. This authorization typically includes the final authority for decisions concerning (1) the employment or termination of staff members, and (2) the facility operation and programming within guidelines established by the parent agency or governing body.

A correctional facility also must have (1) a separate perimeter that precludes the regular commingling of the inmates with inmates from other facilities, (2) a separate facility budget managed by a chief executive officer within guidelines established by the parent agency or governing authority, and (3) staff that is permanently assigned to the facility.

Counseling — Planned use of interpersonal relationships to promote social adjustment. Counseling programs provide opportunities to express feelings verbally with the goal of resolving the individual's problems. At least three types of counseling may be provided: individual, a one-to-one relationship; small group counseling; and large group counseling in a living unit.

County parole — The status of a county jail inmate who, convicted of a misdemeanor and conditionally released from a confinement facility prior to the expiration of sentence, has been placed under supervision in the community for a period of time.

Delinquent act — An act that, if committed by an adult, would be considered a crime.

Delinquent youth — Also referred to as a juvenile delinquent or a criminal-type offender, a youth who has been charged with or adjudicated for conduct that would, under the law of the jurisdiction in which the offense was committed, be a crime if committed by an adult. (See also *Status offender* and *Juvenile*.)

Detainee — Any person confined in a local detention facility not serving a sentence for a criminal offense.

Detainer — A warrant placed against a person in a federal, state, or local correctional facility that notifies the holding authority of the intention of another jurisdiction to take custody of that individual when he or she is released.

Detention warrant — A warrant that authorizes the arrest and temporary detention of a parolee pending preliminary revocation proceedings. A detention warrant should be distinguished from a warrant for the return of a parolee to prison, although return warrants are sometimes used as detainers. For the purpose of these standards, return warrants used as detainers are also deemed to be detention warrants.

Direct supervision — A method of inmate management that ensures continuing direct contact between inmates and staff by posting an officer(s) inside each housing unit. Officers in general housing units are not separated from inmates by a physical barrier. Officers provide frequent, non-scheduled observation of and personal interaction with inmates.

Disciplinary detention — A form of separation from the general population in which inmates committing serious violations of conduct regulations are confined by the disciplinary committee or other authorized group for short periods of time to individual cells separated from the general population. Placement in detention may only occur after a finding of rule violation at an impartial hearing and when there is not adequate alternative disposition to regulate the inmate's behavior. (See also *Protective custody and Segregation*.)

Disciplinary hearing — A nonjudicial administrative procedure to determine if substantial evidence exists to find an inmate guilty of a rule violation.

Dispositional hearing — A hearing held subsequent to the adjudicatory hearing in order to determine what order of disposition (e.g., probation, training school, foster home) should be made concerning a juvenile adjudicated as delinquent.

Diversion — The official halting or suspension, at any legally prescribed point after a recorded justice system entry, of formal criminal or juvenile justice proceedings against an alleged offender. The suspension of proceedings may be in conjunction with a referral of that person to a treatment or care program administered by a nonjudicial agency or a private agency, or there may be no referral.

Due process safeguards — Those procedures that ensure just, equal, and lawful treatment of an individual involved in all stages of the juvenile or criminal justice system, such as a notice of allegations, impartial and objective fact finding, the right to counsel, a written record of proceedings, a statement of any disposition ordered with the reasons for it, and the right to confront accusers, call witnesses, and present evidence.

Education program — A program of formal academic education or a vocational training activity designed to improve employment capability.

Educational release — The designated time when residents or inmates leave the program or institution to attend school in the community and return to custody after school hours.

Emergency — Any significant disruption of normal facility or agency procedure, policy, or activity caused by riot, escape, fire, natural disaster, employee action, or other serious incident.

Emergency care — Care of an acute illness or unexpected health care need that cannot be deferred until the next scheduled sick call. Emergency care shall be provided to the resident population by the medical director, physician, or other staff, local ambulance services, and/or outside hospital emergency rooms. This care shall be expedited by following specific written procedures for medical emergencies described in the standards.

Environmental health — All conditions, circumstances, and surrounding influences that affect the health of individuals or groups in the area.

Facility — A place, institution, building (or part thereof), set of buildings, or area (whether or not enclosing a building or set of buildings) that is used for the lawful custody and/or treatment of individuals. It may be owned and/or operated by public or private agencies and includes the staff and services as well as the buildings and grounds.

Facility administrator — Any official, regardless of local title (e.g., sheriff, chief of police, administrator, warden/superintendent) who has the ultimate responsibility for managing and operating the facility.

Field agency — The unit of a governing authority that has direct responsibility for the provision of field supervision services and for the carrying out of policy as set by the governing authority.

Field services — Services provided to delinquent youth, status offenders, or adult offenders in the community by probation, parole, or other agencies.

Field staff — The professionals assigned case responsibility for control, supervision, and provision of program services to delinquent youth or adult offenders. (Sometimes referred to as field workers.)

First aid — Care for a condition that requires immediate assistance from an individual trained in first aid care and the use of the facility's first aid kits.

Fiscal position control — The process that ensures that individuals on the payroll are legally employed, positions are authorized in the budget, and funds are available.

Footcandle — A unit for measuring the intensity of illumination, defined as the amount of light thrown on a surface one foot away from the light source.

Furlough or *Temporary leave* — A period of time during which a resident is allowed to leave the facility and go into the community unsupervised.

Good-time — A system established by law whereby a convicted offender is credited a set amount of time, which is subtracted from his or her sentence, for specified periods of time served in an acceptable manner.

Governing authority — In public/governmental agencies, the administrative department or division to which the agency reports; the policy-setting body. In private agencies, this may be an administrative headquarters, central unit, or the board of directors or trustees.

Grievance/Grievance process — A circumstance or action considered to be unjust and grounds for complaint or resentment and/or a response to that circumstance in the form of a written complaint filed with the appropriate body.

Handicapped — Having a mental or physical impediment or disadvantage that substantially limits an individual's ability to use programs or services.

Health authority — The physical, health administrator, or agency responsible for the provision of health care services at an institution or system of institutions; the responsible physician may be the health authority.

Health care — The sum of all action taken, preventative and therapeutic, to provide for the physical and mental well-being of a population. Includes medical and dental services, mental health services, nursing, personal hygiene, dietary services, and environmental conditions.

Health care personnel — Individuals whose primary duty is to provide health services to inmates in keeping with their respective levels of health care training or experience.

Health-trained personnel or *Medically-trained personnel* — Correctional officers or other correctional personnel who may be trained and appropriately supervised to carry out specific duties with regard to the administration of health care.

Hearing — A proceeding to determine a course of action, such as the placement of a juvenile or adult offender, or to determine guilt or innocence in a disciplinary matter. Argument, witnesses, or evidence are heard by a judicial officer or administrative body in making the determination.

Hearing examiner — An individual appointed by the parole authority who conducts hearings for the authority. His or her power of decision making may include, but not be limited to, making parole recommendations to granting, denying, or revoking parole.

Holding facility or *Lockup* — A temporary confinement facility, for which the custodial authority is usually less than forty-eight hours, where arrested persons are held pending release, adjudication, or transfer to another facility.

Holidays — All days legally designated as nonworkdays by statute or by the chief governing authority of a jurisdiction.

Independent operator — A person or persons who contracts with a correctional agency or other governmental agency to operate and manage a correctional program or facility.

Independent source — A person, organization, or group that acts independently from the correctional unit being evaluated. An independent source may not be a staff member who reports to the chief executive officer of the unit being audit.

Indigent — An individual with no funds or source of income.

Industries — An activity existing in a correctional system that uses inmate labor to produce goods and/or services for sale. These goods and/or services are sold at prices calculated to recover all or a substantial portion of costs associated with their production and may include a margin of profit. Sale of the products and/or services is not limited to the institution where the industries activity is located.

Information system — The concepts, personnel, and supporting technology for the collection, organization, and delivery of information for administrative use. There are two such types of information: (1) standard information, consisting of the data required for operations control such as the daily count, payroll data in a personnel office, probation/parole success rates, referral sources, and caseload levels; (2) demand information, consisting of information that can be generated when a report is required, such as information on the number of residents in educational and training programs, duration of residence, or the number of residents eligible for discharge during a twelve-month period by offense, sentence, and month of release. (Also referred to as a management information system.)

Informed consent — The agreement by a patient to a treatment, examination, or procedure after the patient receives the material facts regarding the nature, consequences, risks, and alternatives concerning the proposed treatment, examination, or procedure.

Inmate — Any individual, whether in pretrial, unsentenced, or sentenced status, who is confined in a correctional facility.

Institution industries manager — The individual designated as responsible for industries operations at a specific institution in the correctional system.

Interstate compact for the supervision of probationers and parolees — An agreement entered into by eligible jurisdictions in the United States and its territories that provides the criteria for these jurisdictions to cooperate in working with probations and releases.

Interstate compact on juveniles — An agreement authorizing the interstate supervision of juvenile delinquents. This can also include the cooperative institutionalization of special types of delinquent juveniles, such as psychotics and defective delinquents.

Judicial review — A proceeding to reexamine the course of action or continued confinement of a juvenile in a secure detention facility. Arguments, witnesses, or evidence are not required as part of the review. Reviews may be conducted by a judge, judicial officer, or an administrator who has been delegated the authority to release juveniles from secure detention with the approval of the judge.

Juvenile — A person under the age of twenty-one, or as defined in the local jurisdiction as under the age of majority.

Juvenile community residential program — A program housed in a structure without security fences and security hardware or other major restraining construction typically associated with correctional facilities, such as a converted apartment building or private home. They are not constructed as or intended to be detention facilities. Except for daycare programs, they provide twenty-four-hour care, programs, and supervision to juveniles in residence. Their focus is on providing the juvenile with positive adult models and program activities that assist in resolving problems specific to this age group in an environment conducive to positive behavior in the community.

Juvenile day treatment program — A program that provides services to juveniles who live at home and report to the program on a daily basis. Juveniles in these programs require more attention than that provided by probation and aftercare services. Often the program operates its own education program through the local school district. The population is usually drawn from court commitments but may include juveniles enrolled as a preventive or diversionary measure. The program may operate as part of a residential program, and it may provide space for occasional overnight stays by program participants where circumstances warrant additional assistance.

Juvenile detention — Temporary care of juvenile offenders and juveniles alleged to be delinquent who require secure custody in a physically restricting facility.

Juvenile group home — A nonsecure residential program emphasizing family-style living in a homelike atmosphere. Program goals are similar to those for large community residential programs. Although group homes usually house youth who are court-committed, they also house abused or neglected youths who are placed by social agencies. Small group homes serve from four to eight youths; large group homes serve eight to twelve. Their age ranges from ten to seventeen, with the concentration from thirteen to sixteen.

Juvenile intake — The process of determining whether the interests of the public or the juvenile require the filing of a petition with the juvenile court. Generally an intake officer receives, reviews, and processes complaints, recommends detention or release, and provides services for juveniles and their families, including diversion and referral to other community agencies.

Juvenile ranch — A nonsecure residential program providing services to youths in a rural setting. Typically, the residents participate in a structured program of education, recreation, and facility maintenance, including responsibility for the physical plant, its equipment, and livestock. Often there are twenty to sixty juveniles in the ranch setting, ranging in age from thirteen to eighteen.

Life Safety Code — A manual published and updated by the National Fire Protection Association specifying minimum standards for fire safety necessary in the public interest. Two chapters are devoted to correctional facilities.

Major equipment — All equipment that is securely and permanently fastened to the building or any equipment with current book value of $1,000 or more.

Major infraction — A rule infraction involving a grievous loss and requiring imposition of due process procedures. Major infractions include (1) violations that may result in disciplinary detention or administrative segregation; (2) violations for which punishment may tend to increase an inmate's sentence, such as extending parole eligibility; (3) violations that may result in a forfeiture, such as loss of good-time or work time; and (4) violations that may be referred for criminal prosecution.

Medical records — Separate records of medical examinations and diagnoses maintained by the responsible physician. The date and time of all medical examinations and copies of standing or direct medical orders from the physician to the facility staff should be transferred to the resident record.

Medical restraints — Either chemical restraints, such as sedatives, or physical restraints, such as straitjackets, applied only for medical or psychiatric purposes.

Medical screening — A system of structured observation/initial health assessment to identify newly arrived juvenile or adult offenders who pose a health or safety threat to themselves or others.

Mentally retarded — Describes an individual who functions at a subaverage general intellectual level and is deficient in adaptive behavior.

NFPA — National Fire Protection Association. Publishes the *Life Safety Code*.

National uniform parole reports system — A cooperative effort sponsored by the National Parole Institute that calls for the voluntary cooperation of all federal and state authorities having responsibility for felony offenders in developing some common terms to describe parolees — their age, sex, and prior record — and some common definitions to describe parole performance. These types of data allow comparisons across states and other jurisdictions.

Not Applicable — A term used in the accreditation process to describe a standard that does not apply to the correctional unit being audited. While the initial determination of applicability is made by ACA staff and/or the audit team, the final decision rests with the hearing panel.

Offender — An individual convicted or adjudicated of a criminal offense.

Official personnel file — A current and accurate record of the employee's job history, including all pertinent information relating to that history.

Operating unit — One distinct operation of the industries activity, which may be operated as a cost center or separate accounting entity. It may take the form of a manufacturing operation (e.g., furniture making, clothing production), an agricultural operation (e.g., dairy or poultry farming, crop or orchard farming, raising beef or pork), or a service activity (e.g., warehouse, keypunch, microfilming, laundering, auto repair, etc.).

Out-client — An individual who does not live at the facility but who may take advantage of facility services and programs.

Parent — The individual with whom a juvenile regularly lives and who is the natural, adoptive, or surrogate parent.

Parent government organization — Also referred to as a parent agency, the administrative department or division to whom the agency seeking accreditation reports; the policy-setting body.

Parole authority — The decision-making body that has responsibility to grant, deny, and revoke parole. In some jurisdictions it is called the parole board or the parole commission. The term parole authority includes all of these bodies.

Parole hearing — A procedure conducted by a parole authority member and/or hearing examiner in which all pertinent aspects of an eligible inmate's case are reviewed to make a decision or recommendation that would change the inmate's legal status and/or degree of freedom.

Permanent status — A personnel status that provides due process protection prior to dismissal.

Petition — An application for a court order or other judicial action. For example, a delinquency petition is an application for the court to act in the matter of a juvenile apprehended for a delinquent act.

Physical examination — A thorough evaluation of a patient's current physical condition and medical history conducted by or under the supervision of a licensed professional.

Placing authority — The agency or body with the authority to order a juvenile into a specific dispositional placement. This may be the juvenile court, the probation department, or another duly constituted and authorized placement agency, or a contract with service providers for placement services.

Plan of action — A description of action steps designed to correct a condition that has caused a determination of noncompliance with a standard.

Policy — A course or line of action adopted and pursued by an agency that guides and determines present and future decisions and actions. Policies indicate the general course or direction of an organization within which the activities of the personnel must operate. They are statements of guiding principles that should be followed in directing activities toward the attainment of objectives. Their attainment may lead to compliance with standards as well as compliance with the overall goals of the agency or system.

Population center — A geographical area containing at least 10,000 people, along with public safety services, professional services, employment and educational opportunities, and cultural/recreational opportunities.

Preliminary hearing — A hearing at which it is determined whether probable cause exists to support an allegation of parole violation, pending a revocation hearing by the parole authority.

Pretrial release — A procedure whereby an accused individual who had been taken into custody is allowed to be released before and during his or her trial.

Probation — A court-ordered disposition alternative through which a convicted adult offender or an adjudicated delinquent is placed under the control, supervision, and care of a probation field staff member.

Procedure — The detailed and sequential actions that must be executed to ensure that a policy is fully implemented. It is the method of performing an operation or a manner of proceeding on a course of action. It differs from a policy in that it directs action in a particular situation to perform a specific task within the guidelines of policy.

Professional association — A collective body of individuals engaged in a particular profession or vocation. The American Correctional Association, the American Medical Association, and the National Association of Clinical Psychologists are examples of professional associations, of which there are hundreds in the United States.

Professional staff — Social workers, probation officers, and other staff assigned to juvenile and adult offender cases. These individuals generally possess bachelor's degrees and advanced training in the social or behavioral sciences.

Program — The plan or system through which a correctional agency works to meet its goals; often this program requires a distinct physical setting, such as a correctional institution, community residential facility, group home, or foster home.

Program director — The individual directly in charge of the program, who may also be called the administrator, superintendent, or houseparent.

Protective custody — A form of separation from the general population for inmates requesting or requiring protection from other inmates for reasons of health or safety. The inmate's status is reviewed periodically by the classification committee or other designated group. (See *Administrative segregation* and *Disciplinary detention*.)

Records (*juvenile and adult offenders*) — Information concerning the individual's delinquent or criminal, personal, and medical history and behavior and activities while in custody, including but not limited to commitment papers, court orders, detainers, personal property receipts, visitors lists, photographs, fingerprints, type of custody, disciplinary infractions and actions taken, grievance reports, work assignments, program participation, and miscellaneous correspondence.

Referral — The process by which a juvenile or adult offender is introduced to an agency or service that can provide the assistance needed.

Release on bail — The release by a judicial officer of an accused individual who has been taken into custody on the accused's promise to appear in court as required for criminal proceedings.

Releasing authority — The decision-making body and/or individual that has the responsibility to grant, deny, and revoke release from a juvenile institution or program of supervision. In some jurisdictions it is called the parole board or the parole commission. (See *Aftercare.*)

Renovation — A significant structural or design change in the physical plant of a facility.

Responsible physician — An individual licensed to practice medicine and provide health services to the inmate population of the facility and/or the physician at an institution with final responsibility for decisions related to medical judgements.

Revocation hearing — A hearing before the parole authority at which it is determined whether revocation of parole should be made final.

Safety equipment — Primarily firefighting equipment, e.g., chemical extinguishers, hoses, nozzles, water supplies, alarm systems, sprinkler systems, portable breathing devices, gas masks, fans, first aid kits, stretchers, and emergency alarms.

Safety vestibule — In a correctional facility, a grill cage that divides the inmate areas from the remainder of the institution. They must have two doors or gates, only one of which opens at a time, to permit entry to or exit from inmate areas in a safe and controlled manner.

Sally port — An enclosure situated in the perimeter wall or fence of a correctional facility containing gates or doors at both ends, only one of which opens at a time, ensuring there will be no breach in the perimeter security of the institution. The sally port may handle either pedestrian or vehicular traffic.

Secure institution — Any facility that is designed and operated to ensure that all entrances and exits are under the exclusive control of the facility's staff, thereby not allowing an inmate/resident to leave the facility unsupervised or without permission.

Security or Custody — The degree of restriction of inmate movement within a detention/correctional facility, usually divided into maximum, medium, and minimum risk levels.

Security devices — Locks, gates, doors, bars, fences, screens, ceilings, floors, walls, and barriers used to confine and control detained individuals. Also included are electronic monitoring equipment, security alarm systems, security lights, auxiliary power supplies, and other equipment used to maintain facility security.

Security perimeter — The outer portions of a facility that provide for secure confinement of facility inmates/residents. The design of the perimeter may vary depending on the security classification of the facility.

Segregation — The confinement of an inmate to an individual cell that is separated from the general population. There are three forms of segregation: administrative segregation, disciplinary detention, and protective custody.

Self-insurance coverage — A statewide system designed to insure the payment of all legal claims for injury or damage incurred as a result of the actions of state officials, employees, or agents. In public agencies, the self-insurance program is usually authorized by the legislature. A "memorandum of insurance" or similar document is required that acts as a policy, setting the limits of liability for various categories of risk, including deductible limits. Approval of the policy by a cabinet-level official is also required.

Serious incident — A situation in which injury serious enough to warrant medical attention occurs involving a resident, employee, or visitor on the grounds of the institution. Also, a situation containing an imminent threat to the security of the institution and/or to the safety of residents, employees, or visitors on the grounds of the institution.

Severe mental disturbance — A condition in which an individual is a danger to self or others or is incapable of attending to basic physiological needs.

Shelter facility — Any nonsecure public or private facility designated to provide either temporary placement for alleged or adjudicated status offenders prior to the issuance of a disposition order or longer-term care under a juvenile court disposition order.

Sheriff — The elected or appointed chief executive officer of a county law enforcement agency. Sheriffs can serve several functions, including responsibility for law enforcement in unincorporated areas, operation of the county jail, and assignment as officers of the court.

Special management inmate — An individual whose behavior presents a serious threat to the safety and security of the facility, staff, general inmate population, or himself or herself. Special handling and/or housing is required to regulate their behavior.

Special needs inmate — An inmate whose mental and/or physical condition requires special handling and treatment by staff. Special needs inmates include, but are not limited to, drug or alcohol addicts or abusers, the emotionally disturbed, mentally retarded, suspected mentally ill, physically handicapped, chronically ill, and the disabled or infirm.

Status offender — A youth who has been charged with or adjudicated for conduct that under the law of the jurisdiction in which the offense was committed would not be a crime if committed by an adult. (See also *Delinquent youth.*)

Strip search — An examination of an inmate/resident's naked body for weapons, contraband, and physical abnormalities. This also includes a thorough search of all of the individual's clothing while it is not being worn.

Temporary release — A period of time during which an inmate is allowed to leave the program or institution and go into the community unsupervised for various purposes consistent with the public interest.

Training — An organized, planned, and evaluated activity designed to achieve specific learning objectives and enhance the job performance of personnel. Training may occur on site, at an academy or training center, an institution of higher learning, professional meetings, or through contract service or closely supervised on-the-job training. It includes a formal agenda and instruction by a teacher, manager, or official; physical training; or other instruction programs that include a trainer/trainee relationship. Training programs usually include requirements for completion, attendance recording, and a system for recognition of completion. Meetings of professional associations are considered training where there is clear evidence of the above. Whether it occurs on site, at an academy or training center, through contract services, or at professional meetings, the activity must be part of an overall training program.

Training school — Also known as a youth development center, youth village, youth correction center, youth treatment center, youth service center, or school or home for boys and girls. The typical training school may provide supervision, programs, and residential services for more than 100 residents; however, programs of this size are not encouraged. (Standards for new facilities require that each new training school have no more than 100 beds and be limited to two stores in height.) These facilities are designed and operated to be secure institutions.

Youth development centers, youth treatment centers, secure training schools, and other facilities in the category may serve relatively smaller populations ranging from forty to 100 juveniles. The age range served is generally from thirteen to eighteen, although in many jurisdictions residents may be as young as ten or as old as twenty. Older residents are usually juveniles who have been returned to the facility as parole violators.

Treatment plan — A series of written statements that specify the particular course of therapy and the roles of medical and nonmedical personnel in carrying it out. A treatment plan is individualized, based on assessment of the individual patient's needs, and includes a statement of the short- and long-term goals and the methods by which the goals will be pursued. When clinically indicated, the treatment plan provides inmates with access to a range of supportive and rehabilitative services, e.g., individual or group counseling and/or self-help groups that the physician deems appropriate.

Unit management — A management system that subdivides an institution into units. The unit management system has several basic requirements:

1. Each unit holds a relatively small number of inmates. Ideally, there should be less than 150 but not more than 500 inmates.

2. Inmates are housed in the same unit for a major portion of their confinement.

3. Inmates assigned to a unit work in a close relationship with a multidisciplinary team of staff who are regularly assigned to the unit and whose officers are located within the unit.

4. Staff members have decision-making authority for the institutional programming and living conditions for the inmates assigned to the unit within broad rules, policies, and guidelines established by the agency and/or the facility administrator.

5. Inmate assignments to a unit are based on the inmate's need for control, security, and programs offered.

Unit management increases contact between staff and inmates, fosters increased interpersonal relationships, and leads to more knowledgeable decision making as a direct result of staff dealing with a smaller, more permanent group. At the same time, the facility benefits from the economies inherent in centralized service facilities, such as utilities, food service, health care, educational systems, vocational programs, and recreational facilities.

Urine surveillance program — A program whereby urine samples are collected on an irregular basis from offenders suspected of having a history of drug use to determine current or recent use.

Volunteer — An individual who donates his or her time and effort to enhance the activities and programs of the agency. They are selected on the basis of their skills or personal qualities to provide services in recreation, counseling, education, religion, etc.

Waiver — A commission panel decision that releases the correctional unit from the responsibility of preparing a plan of action to being the unit into compliance with a standard.

Warden/Superintendent — The individual in charge of the institution; the chief executive or administrative officer. This position is sometimes referred to by other titles, but warden and superintendent are the most commonly used terms.

Work release — A formal arrangement sanctioned by law whereby an inmate/resident is released into the community to maintain approved and regular employment.

Worker's Compensation — A statewide system of benefits for employees who incur job-related injuries.

The 1870 declaration of principles republished on the following pages was passed by the first Congress of Correction after a three-day discussion of the issues and a thorough review of papers presented by delegates from England, Ireland, Italy, France, and Germany. These principles were discussed and enacted to become the original foundation for ACA standards as we know them today. A total of 329 representatives attended that first Congress from 25 states and Canada. True to the intentions that prevailed during that first Congress, ACA standards have been regularly revised to reflect societal changes as they have occurred. All corrections professionals are indebted to these men and women of vision who, for the first time in recorded history, considered worldwide prison conditions and established the first international prison association that was destined to become the American Correctional Association.

W. Hardy Rauch
Director, Standards and Accreditation
Amercian Correctional Association

First Congress of Correction Participants

President: His Excellency Rutherford B. Hayes, Governor of Ohio

Vice Presidents:

United States	Rev. E.C. Wines, D.D., LL.D.	California	Rev. James Woodworth
Connecticut	E. W. Hatch, M.D.	Illinois	George W. Perkins
Indiana	Gov. Conrad Baker	Iowa	Martin Heisey
Kansas	Hon. E. Hensley	Kentucky	Hon. R. K. White
Maine	Hon. E. G. Harlow	Maryland	G. S. Griffith
Massachusetts	F. B. Sanborn	Michigan	Hon. C. J. Walker
Missouri	Rev. D. A. Wilson	Nebraska	Hon. F. Templin
New Hampshire	Ex-Gov. Frederick Smyth	New Jersey	Ex-Gov. Daniel Haines
New York	Gen. Amos Pilsbury	North Carolina	Hon. G. William Welker
Ohio	Hon. Charles Thomas	Pennsylvania	T. H. Nevin
Rhode Island	E. M. Snow, M.D.	West Virginia	William B. Curtis, M.D.
Wisconsin	Hon. Edwin Hurlbut	Dominion of Canada	William Elder, A.M.
Columbia, South America	Enrique Cortes		

Secretaries: Bradford K. Pierce, D.D., New York

Z. R. Brockway, Michigan
Rev. A. G. Byers, Ohio
Rev. Joshua Coit, Massachusetts

Treasurer: Charles F. Coffin, Indiana

Presiding Officer of Discussion Sessions: Hon. James G. Blaine, Speaker of the U.S. House of Representatives

Guest Presenters to the Congress:

Frederick Merrick, D.D., President of Wesleyan University, Delaware, Ohio
Florence Nightengale, London, England
S. G. Howe, M.D., President, Massachusetts Board State Charities, Boston
M. Bonneville de Marsangy (the Inventor), Counselor of the Imperial Court of Paris, France
Rensselaer N. Hayes, Esq., Member, Board of Managers, New York Juvenile Asylum, New York
Joanna Margaret Hill, Bristol, England
M. Beltrani Scalia, Inspector-General of Prisons in the Kingdom of Italy, Florence, Italy
Baron Franz Von Holzendorff, LL.D., Professor of Law in the Royal University of Berlin, Prussia
Terence J. O'Neil, Esq., Inspector of Prisons in Canada, Toronto, Ontario
Fr. Bruun, Inspector of Prisons in Denmark, Copenhagen
Sir Walter Crofton, C.B., Winchester, England
Sir John Bowring, Claremont, England
Col. G. Y. W. Henderson, Commissioner of Police, London, England
B. F. Wainwright, Superintendent, House of Refuge, Plainfield, Illinois
Mary Carpenter, Superintendent, Red Lodge Reformatory, Bristol, England

Declaration of Principles Adopted and Promulgated by the Congress
October 12 - 18, 1870
Cincinnati, Ohio

I. Crime is an intentional violation of duties imposed by law, which inflicts an injury upon others. Criminals are persons convicted of crime by competent courts.

II. The treatment of criminals by society is for the protection of society. But since such treatment is directed to the criminal rather than to the crime, its great object should be his moral regeneration.

III. The progressive classification of prisoners, based on character and worked on some well-adjusted mark system, should be established in all prisons above the common jail.

IV. Since hope is a more potent agent than fear, it should be made an ever-present force in the minds of prisoners, by a well-devised and skillfully-applied system of rewards for good conduct, industry and attention to learning. Rewards, more than punishments, are essential to every good prison system.

V. The prisoner's destiny should be placed, measurably, in his own hands; he must be put into circumstances where he will be able, through his own exertions, to continually better his own condition. A regulated self-interest must be brought into play, and made constantly operative.

VI. The two master forces opposed to the reform of the prison systems of our several states are political appointments, and a consequent instability of administration. Until both are eliminated, the needed reforms are impossible.

VII. Special training, as well as high qualities of head and heart, is required to make a good prison or reformatory officer. Then only will the administration of public punishment become scientific, uniform and successful, when it is raised to the dignity of a profession, and men are specially trained for it, as they are for other pursuits.

VII. Peremptory sentences ought to be replaced by those of indeterminate length. Sentences limited only by satisfactory proof of reformation should be substituted for those measured by mere lapse of time.

IX. Of all reformatory agencies, religion is first in importance, because most potent in its action upon the human heart and life.

X. Education is a vital force in the reformation of fallen men and women. Its tendency is to quicken the intellect, inspire self-respect, excite to higher aims, and afford a healthful substitute of low and vicious amusements. Education is, therefore, a matter of primary importance in prisons, and should be carried to the utmost extent consistent with the other purposes of such institutions.

XI. In order to the reformation of imprisoned criminals, there must be not only a sincere desire and intention to that end, but a serious conviction, in the minds of the prison officers, that they are capable of being reformed, since no man can heartily maintain a discipline at war with his inward beliefs; no man can earnestly strive to accomplish what in his heart he despairs of accomplishing.

XII. A system of prison discipline, to be truly reformatory, must gain the will of the convict. He is to be amended; but how is this possible with his mind in a state of hostility? No system can hope to succeed, which does not secure this harmony of wills, so that the prisoner shall choose for himself what his officer chooses for him. But, to this end, the officer must really choose the good of the prisoner, and the prisoner must remain in his choice long enough for virtue to become a habit. This consent of wills is an essential condition of reformation.

XIII. The interest of society and the interest of the convicted criminal are really identical, and they should be made practically so. At present there is a combat between crime and laws. Each sets the other at defiance, and, as a rule, there is little kindly felling, and few friendly acts, on either side.

XIV. The prisoner's self-respect should be cultivated to the utmost, and every effort made to give back to him his manhood. There is no greater mistake in the whole compass of penal discipline, than its studied imposition of degradation as a part of punishment. Such imposition destroys every better impulse and aspiration. It crushes the weak, irritates the strong, and indisposes all to submission and reform. It is trampling where we ought to raise, and is therefore as unchristian in principle as it is unwise in policy.

XV. In prison administration, moral forces should be relied upon, with as little admixture of physical force as possible, and organized persuasion be made to take the place of coercive restraint, the object being to make upright and industrious freemen, rather than orderly and obedient prisoners. Brute force may make good prisoners; moral training alone will make good citizens. To the latter of these ends, the living soul must be won; to the former, only the inert and obedient body.

XVI. Industrial training should have both a higher development and a greater breadth than has heretofore been, or is now, commonly given to it in our prisons. Work is no less an auxiliary to virtue, than it is a means of support. Steady, active, honorable labor is the basis of all reformatory discipline. It not only aids reformation, but is essential to it. It was a maxim with Howard, "make men diligent, and they will be honest" -- a maxim which this congress regards as eminently sound and practical.

XVII. While industrial labor in prisons is of the highest importance and utility to the convict, and by no means injurious to the laborer outside, we regard the contract system of prison labor, as now commonly practised in our country, as prejudicial alike to discipline, finance, and the reformation of the prisoner, and sometimes injurious to the interest of the free laborer.

XVIII. The most valuable parts of the Irish prison system--the more strictly penal stage of separate imprisonment, the reformatory stage of progressive classification, and the probationary stage of natural training--are believed to be as applicable to one country as another--to the United States as to Ireland.

XIX. Prisons, as well as prisoners, should be classified or graded so that there shall be prisons for the untried, for the incorrigible and for other degrees of depraved character, as well as separate establishments for women, and for criminals of the younger class.

XX. It is the judgement of this congress, that repeated short sentences for minor criminals are worse than useless; that, in fact, they rather stimulate than repress transgression. Reformation is a work of time; and a benevolent regard to the good of the criminal himself, as well as to the protection of society, requires that his sentence be long enough for reformatory processes to take effect.

XXI. Preventive institutions, such as truant homes, industrial schools, etc., for the reception and treatment of children not yet criminal, but in danger of becoming so, constitute the true field of promise, in which to labor for the repression of crime.

XXII. More systematic and comprehensive methods should be adopted to save discharged prisoners, by providing them with work and encouraging them to redeem their character and regain their lost position in society. The state has not discharged its whole duty to the criminal when it has punished him, nor even when it has reformed him. Having raised him up, it has the further duty to aid in holding him up. And to this end it is desirable that state societies be formed, which shall cooperate with each other in this work.

XXIII. The successful prosecution of crime requires the combined action of capital and labor, just as other crafts do. There are two well-defined classes engaged in criminal operations, who may be called the capitalists and the operatives. It is worthy of inquiry, whether a more effective warfare may not be carried on against crime, by striking at the capitalists as a class, than at the operatives one by one, Certainly, this double warfare should be vigorously pushed, since from it the best results, as regards repressive justice, may be reasonably hoped for.

XXIV. Since personal liberty is the rightful inheritance of every human being, it is the sentiment of this congress that the state which has deprived an innocent citizen of this right, and subjected him to penal restraint, should, on unquestionable proof of its mistake, make reasonable indemnification for such wrongful imprisonment.

XXV. Criminal lunacy is a question of vital interest to society; and facts show that our laws regarding insanity, in its relation to crime, need revision, in order to bring them to a more complete conformity to the demands of reason, justice and humanity; so that, when insanity is pleaded in bar of conviction, the investigation may be conducted with greater knowledge, dignity and fairness; criminal responsibility be more satisfactorily determined; the punishment of the sane criminal be made more sure, and the restraint of the insane be rendered at once more certain and more humane.

XXVI. While this congress would not shield the convicted criminal from the just responsibility of his misdeeds, it arraigns society itself as in no slight degree accountable for the invasion of its rights and the warfare upon its interests, practised by the criminal classes. Does society take all the steps which it easily might, to change, or at least to improve, the circumstances in our social state that lead to crime; or, when crime has been committed, to cure the proclivity to it, generated by these circumstances? It cannot be pretended. Let society, then, lay the case earnestly to its conscience, and strive to mend in both particulars. Offences, we are told by a high authority, must come; but a special woe is denounced against those through whom they come. Let us take heed that that woe fall not upon our head.

XXVII. The exercise of executive clemency in the pardon of criminals is a practical question of grave importance, and of great delicacy and difficulty. It is believed that the annual average of executive pardons from the prisons of the whole county reaches ten percent of their population. The effect of the too free use of the pardoning power is to detract from the certainty of punishment for crimes, and to divert the mind of prisoners from the means supplied for their improvement. Pardons should be issue for one or more of the following reasons, viz.: to release the innocent, to correct mistakes made in imposing the sentence, to relieve such suffering from ill-health as requires release from imprisonment, and to facilitate or reward the real reformation of the prisoner. The exercise of this power should be by the executive, and should be guarded by careful examination as to the character of the prisoner and his conduct in prison. Furthermore, it is the opinion of this congress that governors of states should give to their respective legislatures the reasons, in each case, for their exercise of the pardoning power.

XXVIII. The proper duration of imprisonment for a violation of the laws of society is one of the most perplexing questions in criminal jurisprudence. The present extraordinary inequality of sentences for the same or similar crimes is a source of constant irritation among prisoners, and the discipline of our prisons suffers in consequence. The evil is one for which some remedy should be devised.

XXIX. Prison statistics, gathered from a wide field and skillfully digested, are essential to an exhibition of the true character and working of our prison systems. The collection, collation and reduction to tabulated forms of such statistics can best be effected through a national prison discipline society, with competent working committees in every state, or by the establishment of a national prison bureau, similar to the recently instituted national bureau of education.

XXX. Prison architecture is a matter of grave importance. Prisons of every class should be substantial structures, affording gratification by their design and material to a pure taste, but not costly or highly ornate. We are of the opinion that those of moderate size are best, as regards both industrial and reformatory ends.

XXXI. The construction, organization and management of all prisons should be by the state, and they should form a graduated series of reformatory establishments, being arranged with a view to the industrial employment, intellectual education and moral training of the inmates.

XXXII. As a general rule, the maintenance of penal institutions, above the county jail, should be from the earnings of their inmates, and without cost to the state; nevertheless, the true standard of merit in their management is the rapidity and thoroughness of reformatory effect accomplished thereby.

XXXIII. A right application of the principles of sanitary science in the construction and arrangements of prisons is a point of vital importance. The apparatus for heating and ventilation should be the best that is known; sunlight, air and water should be afforded according to the abundance with which nature has provided them; the rations and clothing should be plain but wholesome, comfortable, and in sufficient but not extravagant quantity; the bedsteads, bed and bedding, including sheets and pillowcases, not costly but decent, and kept clean, well aired and free from vermin; the hospital accommodations, medical stores and surgical instruments should be all that humanity requires and science should supply; and all needed means for personal cleanliness should be without stint.

XXXIV. The principle of the responsibility of parents for the full or partial support of their criminal children in reformatory institutions has been extensively applied in Europe, and its practical working has been attended with the best results. It is worthy of inquiry whether this principle may not be advantageously introduced into the management of our American reformatory institutions.

XXXV. It is our conviction that one of the most effective agencies in the repression of crime would be the enactment of laws by which the education of all the children of the state should be made obligatory. Better to force education upon the people than to force them into prison to suffer for crimes, of which the neglect of education and consequent ignorance have been the occasion, if not the cause.

XXXVI. As a principle that crowns all, and is essential to all, it is our conviction that no prison system can be perfect, or even successful to the most desirable degree, without some central authority to sit at the helm, guiding, controlling, unifying and vitalizing the whole. We ardently hope yet to see all the departments of our preventive, reformatory and penal institutions in each state moulded into one harmonious and effective system; its parts mutually answering to and supporting each other; and the while animated by the same spirit, aiming at the same objects, and subject to the same control; yet without loss of the advantages of voluntary aid and effort, wherever they are attainable.

XXXVII. This congress is of the opinion that, both in the official administration of such a system, and in the voluntary co-operation of citizens therein, the agency of women may be employed with excellent effect.

STANDARDS AND ACCREDITATION STAFF
1976 - 1994

Allison, Jeffrey
Ashburn, Kevin W.
Barry, Regina
Bergsmann, Ilene
Boker, Richard
Boschert, Catherine
Boyd, Lois
Burkhardt, Suzanne
Butler, Deborah
Callies, Joy
Calpin, Laura
Davis, Beverly B.
Dezell, Thomas
Dixon, Alexandreena D.
Dunn, Susan Ainsle
Fetter, Jeroldine
Fosen, Robert H.
Gentilucci, Tracy
Glidden, Brenda
Gooding, Howard M.
Green, Myrna
Greene, John J. III
Greene, Peggy B.
Heflin, Lloyd W.
Howard, Roberta L.
Jeness, Susan
Johnson, Juanita
Johnson, Sharon
Kennedy, Karen
Keesling, Carol
Kushner, Karen L.

Levinson, Robert B.
Lewis-Lloyd, Cynthia
Medley, Grace
Miller, Dodie
Miller, Susan S.
Neagle, Ken
O'Shaughnessy, Jane A.
Powers, Christine E.
Powers, Bettie
Price, Shelly J.
Pritchard, Lynn
Pusateri, Linde
Rauch, W. Hardy
Reimer, Ernest G.
Reusing, Charles R.
Ruppe, Gail
Sechrest, Dale
Seckinger, Joan R.
Shaw, Deborah A.
Shaw, Delores
Slattery, Kerrie
Smalley, Karen
Swahl, Carolyn L.
Tuller, Susan M.
Verdeyen, Robert J.
Vogel, Ruth
Ward, Elizabeth A.
Washington, Jeffrey
West, Jean
White, Stephanie
Zachariah, John K.

MEMBERS OF THE STANDARDS COMMITTEE
1976-1996

Albrecht, Thomas (DC) 1988-1990
Allen, Frederick R. (NY) 1982-1986, 1988-1990
Angelone, Ron (NV) 1986-1988
Atchison, Jim (KY) 1976-1978
Aud, Kenneth J. (MI) 1994-2000
Bailey, Paul E. (NV) 1980-1982
Black, James (CO) 1988-1990
Blake, Gary R. (GA) 1986-1988
Belleque, Lester E. (OR) 1982-1986
Bertrand, Roma (CN) 1984-1986
Braithwaite, John W. (CN) 1976-1980
Branham, Lynn S. (IL) 1990-1992
Breaux, Donald J. (LA) 1992-1994
Breed, Allen F. (DC) 1976-1982
Brown, Melvin, Jr. (TX) 1992-1998
Brown, Robert, Jr. (MI) 1988-1990
Brutsche, Robert L. (CA) 1988-1994
Campbell, Nancy M. (WA) 1986-1988
Carlson, Norman A. (DC) 1976-1978
Chamberlain, Norman F. (WA) 1980-1982
Clute, Penelope D. (NY) 1988-1990
Cocoros, John A. (TX) 1990-1992
Coleman, Ray (WA) 1986-1988
Collins, William C. (WA) 1984-1986
Coughlin, Thomas A. (NY) 1988-1994
Crist, Roger W. (CO) 1982-1984
Crawford, Jacqueline (AZ) 1976-1992
Davis, Pamela Jo (FL) 1986-1990
Decell, Grady A. (SC) 1979-1982
Dismukes, Hugh C. (TX) 1980-1982
Dorsey, Helen Brown (WA) 1982-1984
Dorsey, Neil (MD) 1982-1984
Enomoto, J.J. (CA) 1979-1980
Estelle, W.J., Jr. (TX) 1976-1980
Evans, David C. (GA) 1988-1990
Farkas, Gerald M. (DC) 1978-1986
Farrier, Harold A. (IA) 1986-1992
Gagnon, John R. (WI) 1976-1980
Gamby, Jacqueline Jones (CO) 1980-1986
Gaudio, Anthony C. (VA) 1976-1978
Giesen, Linda (IL) 1982-1984
Gispert, Ana (FL) 1982-1984
Goodall, Paula (OK) 1982-1984
Guillen, Rudy F. (VA) 1976-1982
Hahn, Paul H. (OH) 1984-1986
Hawk, Kathleen M. (DC) 1992-2000
Hill, Gary (NE) 1976-1980
Holden, Tamara (UT) 1986-1988
Housewright, Vernon G. (IL) 1976-1982, 1984-1986
Humphrey-Barnett, Susan (AK) 1988-1992
Irving, James R. (IL) 1988-1994
Jackson, Ronald G. (TX) 1978-1980
Johnson, Perry M. (MI) 1984-1992
Jordan, James M. (IL) 1986-1988

Kehoe, Charles J. (MI) 1978-1982
Kelly, Marton (OH) 1976-1978
Lehman, Joseph D. (PA) 1994-1996
Lejins, Peter P. (MD) 1976-1978
Livingston, Shirley H. (FL) 1976-1979
Manley, Harry A. (MD) 1990-1996
Maynard, Gary D. (OK) 1989-1992
McCartt, John M. (OH) 1976-1978
McCotter, O.L. (TX) 1984-1986
McMahon, John F. (NY) 1976-1978
Milliken, William V. (UT) 1982-1984
Minor, John (MI) 1992-1994
Mitchell, Anabel P. (FL) 1984-1986
Moore, Margaret A. (PA) 1990-1996
Morton, Joann B. (SC) 1976-1980
Myers, Victoria C. (MO) 1980-1994
Natalucci-Persichetti, Geno (OH) 1994-2000
Nelson, Ray (CO) 1984-1986
Pappert, Ruth M. (IL) 1980-1982
Parrish, David (FL) 1992-1998
Patrick, Allen L. (OH) 1992-1994
Peters, Howard A. III (IL) 1992-1998
Petrovsky, Joseph (MO) 1982-1984
Phyfer, George M. (AL) 1976-1978
Pointer, Donald W. (MD) 1978-1980
Pugh, Julian U. (VA) 1978-1980
Quinlan, Michael J. (DC) 1986-1990
Rapp, Marcella (CO) 1984-1986
Rees, John D. (LA) 1988-1992
Robinson, Carl (CT) 1982-1984
Robinson, William B. (PA) 1980-1984
Robuck, Lucille (KY) 1976-1978
Rosser, Paul (GA) 1984-1986
Rossi, Linda D'Amario (RI) 1980-1982
Shirley, Sue (TX) 1980-1982
Shope, John T. (NC) 1976-1978
Schmidt, Robert (DC) 1986-1988
Shumate, Denis (KS) 1990-1996
Simonet, John (CO) 1990-1994
Singletary, Harry (FL) 1988-1994
Sipos, Chiquita (CA) 1984-1986, 1992-1998
Sublett, Samuel J. (IL) 1976-1986
Swanson, Virginia (WA) 1988-1990, 1992-1994
Vassar, B. Norris (VA) 1986-1988
Vigil, Celedonio (NM) 1990-1996
Ward, Frederick J. (NJ) 1976-1978
Weber, J. Robert (NC) 1982-1984
Weldon, Paul I. (SC) 1978-1980
White, William S. (IL) 1986-1988
Wilson, George W. (OH) 1988-1990
Wirkler, Norman E. (CO) 1988-1990, 1992-1998
Wrenshall, Allen F. (CN) 1982-1984
Young, Marjorie H. (GA) 1986-1988, 1990-1992

MEMBERS OF THE COMMISSION ON ACCREDITATION FOR CORRECTIONS
1974 - 1996

Ackermann, John (NY) 1976-1977
Black, James (CO) 1986-1988*
Blake, Gary (MD) 1979-1984
Braithwaite, John (CN) 1980-1986
Branham, Lynn S. (IL) 1990-1996
Breaux, Donald J. (LA) 1990-1996
Brutsche, Robert L. (VA) 1986-1998
Charters, Paul (FL) 1979-1984
Clute, Penelope D. (NY) 1984-1990
Coate, Alfred B. (MT) 1975-1980
Cocoros, John (TX) 1988-1994
Coleman, Raymond J. (WA) 1984-1990
Crawford, Jacqueline (AZ) 1986-1992
Cunningham, Su (TX) 1992-1998
Dietz, Christopher D. (NJ) 1980-1986
Dunbar, Walter (NY) 1974-1975
Dunning, James (VA) 1990-1996
Elias, Al (NJ) 1979-1980
Elrod, Richard J. (IL) 1984-1986
Enomoto, J.J. (CA) 1980-1986
Evans, David C. (GA) 1988-1990
Fant, Fred D. (NJ) 1974-1978
Farkas, Gerald M. (PA) 1974-1978
Fryer, Gordon L. (IL) 1974-1978
George, B. James, Jr. (NY) 1979-1984
Gladstone, William E. (FL) 1981-1986
Goodrich, Edna L. (WA) 1978-1982
Green, Leslie R. (MN) 1979-1984
Hammergren, Donald R. (MN) 1975-1979
Hays, Bonnie L. (OR) 1987-1992
Heard, John (TX) 1974-1978
Heyne, Robert P. (IN) 1974-1977
Hopkins, Wayne (DC) 1974-1977
Huggins, M. Wayne (VA) 1983-1988*
Irving, James R. (IL) 1981-1986
Jackson, Ron (TX) 1990-1996
Jackson, Ronald W. (GA) 1992-1998
Jefferson, Ralph A. (WI) 1978-1983
Johnson, Perry M. (MI) 1986-1992
Jordan, James M. (IL) 1984-1996
Kehoe, Charles J. (MD) 1983-1988
Lucas, William (MI) 1978-1983
Maciekowich, Z.C. (AZ) 1974-1975
Mangogna, Thomas J. (MO) 1974-1979

Martinez, Orlando L. (CO) 1986-1992
Maynard, Gary M. (OK) 1990-1994
McGough, John (WA) 1979-1984
Minor, John (MI) 1988-1994
Moeller, H.G. (NC) 1974-1980
Moore, Edgar C. (Ted) (SC) 1982-1988*
Morrissey, Thomas H. (NC) 1979-1980
Myers, Victoria C. (MO) 1982-1994
Newberger, Jay M. (SD) 1984-1990
Nichols, R. Raymond (ME) 1974-1976
Nuernberger, W.W. (NE) 1974-1979
Omodt, Don (MN) 1979-1980
Orlando, Frank A. (FL) 1986-1992
Parsons, Michael (OK) 1994-2000
Patrick, Allen L. (OH) 1990-1996
Patterson, Wayne K. (CO) 1978-1983
Phyfer, George M. (AL) 1986-1998
Pointer, W. Donald (MD) 1974-1977
Quinn, Luke (MI) 1988-2000
Ramirez, Teresa V. (TX) 1994-2000
Rapp, Marcella C. (CO) 1977-1982
Reed, Amos E. (NC) 1976-1981
Riedman, Irvin M. (ND) 1975-1980
Rodriguez, Felix (NM) 1979-1980
Rossi, Linda D'Amario (RI) 1981-1986
Rowan, Joseph R. (IL) 1974-1980
Shirley, Sue (TX) 1981-1986
Simonet, John (CO) 1990-1996
Singletary, Harry (FL) 1992-1998
Skoler, Daniel (DC) 1974-1979
Stalder, Richard (LA) 1994-2000
Swanson, Virginia (WA) 1984-1998
Tremont, J. Steven (LA) 1977-1982
Van DeKamp, John (CA) 1974-1976
Watson, Robert J. (OR) 1977-1982
Weber, J. Robert (KY) 1974-1981
Webster, Marjorie (NH) 1992-1998
Wheeler, Martha E. (MI) 1974-1977
White, William S. (IL) 1983-1988
Wilson, George W. (KY) 1982-1988*
Wirkler, Norman E. (CO) 1984-1990
Young, Marjorie H. (GA) 1986-1998
Youngken, Michael (KS) 1994-2000

*Based on an extension of original term in order to correspond with ACA election year.

THE AMERICAN CORRECTIONAL ASSOCIATION
BOARD OF GOVERNORS MEMBERS
DURING THE STANDARDS AND ACCREDITATION ERA
1974-1996

Adamek, F. Jerald (CO) 1976-1978
Adams, Betty K. (TN) 1990-1994
Agee, Vicki L. (OH) 1986-1988
Andersen, Carolyn (UT) 1984-1986
Anderson, Charles (ID) 1974-1975
Anderson, Judy C. (SC) 1992-1996
Avery, Dennis (MN) 1988-1990, 1992-1994
Avery, Michael T. (TX) 1975-1976
Barker, Marjorie H. (IN) 1976-1980
Barrington, R.W. (CN) 1976-1978
Bergen, Donna R. (MO) 1986-1988
Belleque, Les (OR) 1980-1984
Beto, George (TX) 1974-1976
Bills, John D. (ID) 1974-1976
Bishop, Frank B. III (VA) 1980-1984
Black, James T. (DC) 1980-1982
Black, Lee Roy (MO) 1984-1988
Black, Raymond M. (CA) 1975-1976
Blanchard, Don E. (UT) 1986-1988
Blanton, Jack V. (FL) 1974-1976
Bowman, Jon G. (WA) 1978-1980
Boyle, Edward C. (CA) 1974-1976
Brahe, Champ K. (FL) 1978-1980
Braithwaite, John W. (CN) 1974-1975
Breed, Allen F. (CA) 1974-1976, 1984-1988
Breslin, Maurice (OH) 1974-1975
Brewer, Ernesteen (TN) 1974-1975
Briscoe, Judy Culpepper(TX) 1988-1996
Brown, James W. (IL) 1990-1994
Brown, Robert Jr. (MI) 1988-1990
Bruce, Ronald D. (ID) 1976-1978
Bryant, Robert C. (KY) 1975-1976
Byrd, John W. (TX) 1986-1988
Cain, Robert D. Jr. (AZ) 1976-1980
Callahan, Thomas J. (CA) 1984-1986
Campbell, John D. (NC) 1974-1978
Carlson, Norman A. (DC) 1974-1982
Casas, Anthony (CA) 1982-1984
Case, John (PA) 1974-1975
Cass, E.R. (NY) 1974-1976
Charters, Paul J. (FL) 1975-1980
Chunn, Gwendolyn C. (NC) 1992-1996
Ciuros, William Jr. (NY) 1984-1988
Cocoros, John A. (TX) 1982-1984
Coffey, Betsy (KY) 1982-1986
Colvin, Kaye H. (CO) 1974-1978
Cooper, Bennett J. (OH) 1975-1976, 1982-1992
Corbett, Gary (C)) 1976-1978
Corrothers, Helen G. (DC) 1980-1994
Crawford, Fred L. (FL) 1988-1990
Crawford, Jacqueline (AZ) 1975-1976, 1980-1982
Cunningham, Chester R. (CN) 1982-1986
Cunningham, Su (TX) 1982-1990
Davis, Mary C. (NY) 1976-1978

Davis, Pamela Jo (FL) 1988-1990
Davis, Rendell A (PA) 1984-1986
Decell, Grady A. (SC) 1978-1980
DeHart, Doris (VA) 1980-1982
Denton, George (OH) 1974-1975
Dunlap, Earl L. (KY) 1986-1988
Dye, Larry L. (NY) 1988-1990
Eastland, Charles (KY) 1978-1980
Emmelhainz, Edgar Jr. (FL) 1976-1978
Erickson, Don R. (ID) 1974-1978
Estelle, W.J. Jr. (TX) 1975-1980
Evan, Mary Ann (OR) 1976-1978
Evans, Walter(OR) 1975-1976
Farkas, Gerald M. (MD) 1980-1982
Ferris, Jane (MD) 1976-1978
Freeman, Robert A. (WA) 1974-1978
Gable, Katherine (MA) 1976-1978
Gagnon, John R. (WI) 1978-1980
Gaudio, Anthony (VA) 1976-1978
Gispert, Ana I. (FL) 1984-1990
Gondles, James A. Jr. (VA) 1986-1990, 1992-1994
Gubbins, Edmund (CT) 1974-1975
Guillen, Rudy (VA) 1975-1976
Hahn, Paul H. (OH) 1976-1978, 1982-1984
Hall, Frank A. (MD) 1982-1984
Hammergren, Donald R. (MN) 1974-1975, 1982-1984
Hardesty, George A. (KY) 1976-1978, 1980-1982
Hatrak, Robert S. (NV) 1982-1984
Hill, Gary (NE) 1974-1976, 1982-1984
Hill, Jerry D. (CA) 1986-1988
Holden, Tamara (OR) 1990-1994
Hopkins, Arnold J. (MD) 1984-1996
Howard, Ray E. (FL) 1975-1976
Housewright, Vernon G. (IL) 1975-1980
Hunter, Susan M. (DC) 1984-1986
Hubanks, Allan C. (FL) 1974-1975
Hughes, Gail (MO) 1974-1975, 1990-1996
Huskey, Bobbie L. (IL) 1984-1986, 1988-1994
Hutto, T. Don (TN) 1982-1988
Jackson, Ronald G. (TX) 1978-1980
Johnson, Perry M. (MI) 1980-1984, 1990-1994
Johnson, Terry L. (OR) 1974-1975
Kehoe, Charles J. (MI) 1974-1975, 1978-1982
Kehoe, John (CA) 1974-1975
Keller, Oliver J. (FL) 1974-1978
Killinger, George G. (TX) 1980-1982
Koenning, Keith A. (CO) 1975-1978
Kuharich, Anthony S. (IL) 1974-1978
Kyle, James F. (TN) 1994-1998
Lawrence, James J. (OH) 1994-1998
Leeke, William D. (SC) 1974-1980
Lejins, Peter P. (MD) 1974-1976
Lightsey, Michael (TX) 1976-1978

PRESIDENTS OF THE AMERICAN CORRECTIONAL ASSOCIATION
1870 - 1996

Rutherford B. Hayes, Ohio 1870-1873
H. Seymour, New York 1873-1876
Rutherford B. Hayes, Ohio 1876-1892
R. Brinkerhoff, Ohio 1982-1897
Z.R. Brockway, New York 1897-1898
R.W. McClaugery, Illinois 1898-1899
E. S. Wright, Pennsylvania 1899-1900
J.F. Scott, Massachusetts 1900-1901
C.R. Henderson, Illinois 1901-1902
H. Wolfer, Minnesota 1902-1903
C.T. Lewis, New York 1903-1904
A. Garvin, Connecticut 1904-1905
C.V. Collins, New York 1905-1906
E.G. Murphy, Illinois 1906-1907
J.L. Milligan, Pennsylvania 1907-1908
J.T. Gilmour, Canada 1908-1909
A.W. Butler, Indiana 1909-1910
T.B. Patton, Pennsylvania 1910-1911
F.G. Pettigrove, Massachusetts 1911-1912
J.A. Leonard, Ohio 1912-1913
S.G. Smith, Minnesota 1913-1914
J.P. Byers, New Jersey 1914-1915
A. Pratt, Utah 1915-1916
D.C. Peyton, Indiana 1916-1918
B.M. Spurr, West Virginia 1918-1919
G.W. Wickersham, New York 1919-1920
C.B. Adams, Illinois 1920-1921
H.H. Hart, New York 1921-1922
L.E. Lawes, New York 1922-1923
C.H. Johnson, New York 1923-1924
Frank Moore, New Jersey 1924-1925
Sanford Bates, Massachusetts 1925-1926
W.F. Penn, Pennsylvania 1926-1927
E.R. Cass, New York 1927-1928
G.C. Erskine, Connecticut 1928-1929
C.J. Swendsen, Minnesota 1929-1930
L.C. Faulkner, New York 1930-1931
Oscar Lee, Wisconsin 1931-1932
W.N. Thayer Jr., New York 1932-1933
Calvin Derrick, New Jersey 1933-1934
S.P. Ashe, Pennsylvania 1934-1935
B.L. La Du, Illinois 1935-1936
William J. Ellis, New Jersey 1936-1937
Rice M. Youell, Virginia 1937-1938
A.H. MacCormick, New York 1938-1939
J.V. Bennett, District of Columbia 1939-1940

James A. Johnston, California 1940-1941
G. Howland Shaw, District of Columbia 1941-1942
Richard A. McGee, Washington 1942-1943
Joseph W. Sanford, Georgia 1943-1944
Garrett Heyns, Michigan 1944-1945
Sam A. Lewisohn, New York 1945-1946
Harold E. Donnell, Maryland 1946-1947
W. Frank Smyth Jr., Virginia 1947-1948
John C. Burke, Wisconsin 1948-1949
J. Stanley Sheppard, New York 1949-1950
Joseph E. Ragen, Illinois 1950-1951
James W. Curran, Maryland 1951-1952
Ralph B. Gibson, Canada 1952-1953
Walter M. Wallack, New York 1953-1954
Kenyon J. Scudder, California 1954-1955
Myrl E. Alexander, District of Columbia 1955-1956
E. Preston Sharp, Pennsylvania 1956-1957
Roberts J. Wright, New York 1957-1958
O.B. Ellis, Texas 1958-1959
Rev. Gervase Brinkman, Illinois 1959-1960
Sanger B. Powers, Wisconsin 1960-1961
Arthur T. Prasse, Pennsylvania 1961-1962
Peter P. Lejins, Maryland 1962-1963
Harry C. Tinsley, Colorado 1963-1964
Donald Clemmer, District of Columbia 1964-1965
Harold V. Langolis, Rhode Island 1965-1966
Walter Dunbar, District of Columbia 1966-1967
Parker L. Hancock, New Hampshire 1967-1968
Ellis C. MacDougall, Connecticut 1968-1969
Dr. George Beto, Texas 1969-1970
Louie L. Wainwright, Florida 1970-1971
Maurice H. Sigler, District of Columbia 1971-1972
Martha E. Wheeler, Ohio 1972-1973
Joseph S. Coughlin, Illinois 1973-1974
John W. Braithwaite, Canada 1974-1975
Oliver J. Keller, Florida 1975-1976
William D. Leeke, South Carolina 1976-1978
Norman A. Carlson, District of Columbia 1978-1980
Amos E. Reed, North Carolina 1980-1982
H.G. Moeller, North Carolina 1982-1984
T. Don Hutto, Tennessee 1984-1986
Su Cunningham, Texas 1986-1988
Samuel Sublett Jr., Illinois 1988-1990
Helen G. Corrothers, Maryland 1990-1992
Perry M. Johnson, Michigan 1992-1994
Bobbie L. Huskey, Illinois 1994-1996

Index

PROPOSAL FOR STANDARD REVISION

This official proposal form is to be used for changes to all ACA standards manuals. Following completion of the proposal form, it will be presented to the Standards Committee at the next meeting. Proposals to be considered after August 1, 1992 must be made in accordance with the following guidelines.

    I. Manual - Insert the name of each manual to which you believe the changes will apply.
    II. Edition - Insert the edition number(s) of all applicable manuals.
    III. Standard Number(s) - Insert all numbers that apply to your proposal.
    IV. Agency/Facility
        A. Size of Facility - State the size of the facility you operate and/or work in.
        B. Size of Agency - State the total size of your agency.
    V. Date of Proposal

I. Manual	II. Edition
III. Existing Standard Number(s) IV. Agency/Facility A. Size of Facility: B. Size of Agency:	V. Date of Proposal

VI. Type of Proposal (check appropriate box) ❑ New Standard   ❑ Revision   ❑ Deletion

VII. Existing Standard (insert complete standard and existing discussion/comment; a photocopy is preferable)

_____
_____
_____
_____
_____
_____
_____
_____
_____
_____
_____
_____
_____
_____
_____
_____
_____
_____
_____
_____

VIII. Proposal (state the standard and discussion exactly as you believe it should appear in the manual; proposal must be in the same format and worded precisely)

_____
_____
_____
_____
_____
_____
_____
_____
_____
_____
_____
_____
_____

Proposed Discussion/Comment

_____
_____
_____
_____
_____
_____
_____

IX. Impact Statements - It is imperative that all standards be developed after careful consideration of the impact the action will have on staffing, budget, programs, construction, and legal/legislative activities. In each category, state the numbers as exactly as possible, and cite data sources.

A.   Staffing

1. On the Facility

_____
_____
_____
_____

2. On the Agency

_____
_____
_____
_____

B. Annual Budget

    1. On the Facility

_____

_____

_____

_____

    2. On the Agency

_____

_____

_____

_____

C. Program

_____

_____

_____

_____

_____

_____

_____

D. Construction (describe the impact your proposal may have on the physical plant)

_____

_____

_____

_____

_____

_____

E. Legal/Legislative

_____

_____

_____

_____

_____

_____

X. General Comments (explain in your own words why you believe the action should be taken)

_____
_____
_____
_____
_____
_____
_____
_____
_____
_____
_____
_____
_____

Submitted by (name and title) _____

Signature _____

Agency _____

Address _____

City _____ State _____ Zip _____

Telephone (include area code) _____ FAX _____

Forward to:

American Correctional Association
Standards and Accreditation Department
Attn: Standards Coordinator
8025 Laurel Lakes Court
Laurel, Maryland 20707-5075